ACE YOUR C-SUITE INTERVIEW

International Headhunter Reveals
Insider Strategies for Executive Job
Search, Tips to Master Interviewing,
Negotiating Better Salaries and Getting
Hired Fast!

Leora Bach, CPA

Ordering Information

Special discounts are available on quantity purchases by corporations, associations, and other organizations. For details, contact Leora Bach at lbach@bach-associates.com or visit the website at: www.bach-associates.com.

Acknowledgements

Writing a book feels like the most daunting and isolating project, filled with ever present fears. Will people want to read it? Will it be good enough? Will it help my target audience? In fact, it is a very lonely process when you are writing every single word yourself. Then you realize that from inception to publishing, it requires an entire team; no one ever does it alone.

Indeed, I have so many people to thank; I almost don't know where to start. So, I'll start with the people who first suggested that I write this book, my Candidates who years ago kept asking for this book so that they could always have, first hand all the tips and strategies that I gave them in my private coaching sessions with them.

Thank you to all of you, you taught me so much, and your questions kept me on my toes and never made me stop honing my craft - you were all my teachers. I am so grateful for the privilege of meeting you and the experiences that you gave me. Without you, this book would never have been written.

Thank you to Mike Koenigs, Ed Rush, and Pam Hendrickson, you are the most incredibly creative, talented, kind, and generous triumvirate I have ever met. Working with you has changed my life.

Thank you also to Erin Marshall for your prompt and caring Customer Support, you rock! To Chris Hendrickson for your efficiency, kindness, and professionalism - you are irreplaceable.

The rest of the team at Traffic Geyser and The Pulse Network: Patricia Watts for always being so efficient and prompt, Julie Kroupa for your professionalism and excellent customer service, and Megan for your Marketing genius.

To the many people behind the scenes at the above mentioned companies, who I have never met, but whose hard work and diligence I have been the grateful recipient of, my heartfelt thanks to you.

Thank you to Benjamin Payne for the beautiful design and cover of this book; you are so talented and an absolute joy to work with!

To the inimitable Randy Glasbergen for the brilliant and hilarious cartoons; I am so thrilled to have met you through your art.

Thank you to $uper Mario Fachini for always believing in me; your gentle, steadfast encouragement kept me going - you are more than a coach and a mentor to me, you are my hero!

A special thank you to Jason P Jordan and Rory Carruthers for your assistance with the international launch of this book and to Carly Carruthers for editing - your collaboration has been invaluable.

An enormous and heartfelt thank you to Sandra Merk, my colleague, friend and "right hand" for the final edits and endless changes to the Manuscript; I could never have done this without you!

No one is an expert in all things, including myself. When it came to the Social Media aspect of assisting Candidates and advising them in this arena, I turned to two experts - Joshua Waldman and Shanna Landolt.

Thank you both so much for your generous support and excellent advice. Your expertise made an immeasurable difference.

I would like to thank my Clients and Candidates for their testimonials; the gift of their time and most generous comments; you allow those that don't yet know me to see me through your light, and may that light give *them* hope!

Thank you to all my family and friends for their constant encouragement and support and to my mother, Olga, for being there every step of the way. Mom, thank you so much for all the love and support, and for being my sounding board - you are still one of the smartest people I know!

Dedication

To my late father, Max Bach - you were the perfect embodiment of unconditional love, and you remain the most brilliant, generous, kind and enlightened man I have ever known.

I am so honored to be your daughter.

Testimonials

I have had the fortunate experience of being associated with Leora for many years, both as a Candidate and a Client. I am delighted that she is now sharing her extensive knowledge and insights with you in *Ace Your C-Suite Interview*.

Leora guided me as I embarked on an interview for my first C-Suite role, ensuring that I fully understood her Client's needs and the culture of the organization. By investing time and effort to get to know me, both as a professional and an individual, and to fully understand the Client's needs, Leora ensured that the result would be a "win" for Client and Candidate.

This approach was replicated when I was the Client looking for the right Candidate. Another "win-win" result!

One of the key attributes of a great recruiting result is the "fit" between Client and Candidate.

Understanding the needs and culture of the organization, the style and skills of the Candidate, and getting the right combination is where Leora excels.

I am confident that her insights will prove invaluable as you move into *your* next C-Suite role.

W. Alan Ahlgren, CPA, CA
Chief Financial Officer and Corporate Secretary
Graphite One Resources, Inc.

***

When I first called Leora out of the blue, she immediately made helping my career a priority and gave so much of her time.

Leora's sincere desire to coach and unwavering commitment to see me through to landing a stellar position is something I won't ever forget!

I cannot thank her enough for all her help and encouragement; I am looking forward to her publish date!

Cameron MacKenzie
Investment Advisor
RBC Dominion Securities

* * *

If I ever had to get married again, I'd hire Leora to find the right spouse. Her attention to detail and her intense interest in both the Client's and the Candidate's needs has resulted in three excellent Executive additions to my former team.

She was concerned enough to come all the way from North America of her own volition to present Candidates to me in Vietnam!

Leora is a clever lady with a great personality and a good dollop of women's intuition.

The world needs more professional Executive Headhunters like her!

Charles Barclay
Former Chief Operating Officer
Olympus Pacific Minerals Limited

* * *

As CEO of a junior mining Company, I needed to hire our first CFO, and Leora came highly recommended to assist.

Our tall order was to find, with a tight budget in the midst of a rising commodity boom, an entrepreneurial, broadly experienced, self-starter with strong resource experience who could build the position from the ground up and fit into our team.

She deftly guided us through a global search process, minimized our distractions, culled bright-looking prospects that dimmed with reference and background checks and delivered with outstanding success.

This experience, and others that followed, proved to me that Leora Bach is the "go to" resource for Executive Search.

Doug Smith
Former President, CEO & Director
First Coal Corporation

***

In 2008, Leora approached me to see if I was interested in the position of "Group Metallurgist" at Olympus Pacific Minerals Inc. in Vietnam. Following discussions with Leora, it became clear to me that the position was a very good fit for my qualifications.

Leora made sure she understood my expectations for the position and provided invaluable feedback liaising with the Client on my behalf. This ultimately resulted in a successful job interview.

Leora not only helped me in securing the position at Olympus Pacific, but has also followed up with me for feedback so that she can continue to offer the best assistance possible for future Candidates.

Erik Devuyst
Former Group Metallurgist
Olympus Pacific Minerals Ltd.

***

My email to Leora when I heard about this book was:

"I can't think of a better person to be providing this information. Everyone who's worked with you knows you're a star – now the world will as well".

Leora's guidance won me a plum position when we met in the early 90s, and we've kept in touch ever since. Her knowledge of the executive interview process is vast.

She's seen and heard it all, and she understands the nuances and subtleties of managing the Interviewer personalities as well as making a position-winning presentation. She's like a ship's pilot who comes aboard and guides the billion dollar vessel through complex waters to a successful landing.

John H. Dawe, CFA
Chief Financial Officer, Secretary & Treasurer
KonaRed Corporation

***

I am not surprised Leora has written a book providing Candidates an in depth understanding of the "Executive Search Process" and more specifically "How to Ace their C-Suite Interview."

In many cases, Candidates seeking new career opportunities are doing so following the interruption of a career and find themselves in an atmosphere of uncertainty and fear.

Leora has an incredible understanding of people, specifically in this very personal and unsettling time in the Candidates' lives. Her ability to empathize with Candidates and her vast experience in finding "the right Candidates" for Corporate Clients are invaluable to both parties.

She never loses sight of the fact that to be successful, both the Candidate and the Company must win!

I have the unique experience of having had both her assistance and guidance while I personally sought career change as well as her expertise in finding Candidates to fill key roles within the organization I worked for.

She provides successful solutions to challenging situations and conducts her "Search Criteria" to the highest professional standards possible.

Fred Nelson
Director of Operations
The Wood Group

***

I have known Leora Bach for 17 years, and she has always been a shining light for me when it comes to her Integrity, Coaching, and her ability to exhaustively research positions to find the best incumbent, complete with meticulous reports to ensure successful interviews.

If she puts someone forward, I know that this is the best person for the role, and she has also made sure that the Candidate fits the Corporate Culture. Her mentorship of the incumbent cuts to the chase and removes the inefficiencies of the interview process.

With this background, her giving us the Secrets in her book *Ace Your C-Suite Interview* will not only help the Candidate come across at their best, but ensure the Company gets the best Executive for the position. Everyone in the C-Suite must read this book!

Roland Vetter
Chief Financial Officer
Conventus Energy

***

Surely one of the most important things in the interview process is caring about both the Candidate and the Client, a quality Leora has in spades.

This coupled with her innate curiosity, a punishing work ethic, and just being fun to be around easily made her my Headhunter of choice.

Leora's hand-picked Candidates were standout choices in a really tough market, where attracting and retaining Executive talent was immensely difficult.

So to hear of this book, more timely than ever in today's job market, just underlines all of those marvelous qualities.

Then comes the hours and hours paid at the coalface of working in the Executive Search industry and thousands of interviews later to earn those hard won insights we'd all love to get.

Well, here they are! Enjoy these insights from someone at the very top of her game!

Richard Bolleurs
Former, Financial Director
Komatsu South Africa
Subsidiary of Anglo American

***

Leora Bach is the consummate professional. She comes to each meeting fully prepared and versed in the Candidates she is presenting, the market she is serving, and the position she needs to fill.

Her keen understanding of people gives her the ability to match not just credentials with a position but also the right personality with the Company.

I was very impressed with her knowledge of our industry and with the Candidates she was able to attract. Even in a stressful and difficult situation with last minute scheduling changes on an international trip, she managed to ensure that the interviews ran smoothly and the trip was a success.

Leora works very hard at what she does, and she is truly committed to doing the best she can for her Clients.

Julie Van Baarsen, CA
Former CFO
Petaquilla Minerals Ltd.

***

To provide a testimonial for Leora Bach is such an honor; there are not enough words I can say to show my great esteem towards what Leora has done for my career and me personally.

I have known Leora for over 15 years, and every conversation with her is like a gift for me: her unique ability to recognize, understand, and explain complex business and personal relationships has changed my thinking in a much more resourceful and positive way which, most importantly, has influenced my actions and enabled me to make informed decisions and choices in my career.

The advice she has given me has also either dovetailed or reinforced what I know about how I need to change my behaviors.

During a darker time of a difficult career situation a few years ago when I felt I was at the bottom, Leora provided me that voice that came without any personal agenda or political spin that I could trust. She provided a flat wall that I could bounce ideas off with complete openness.

She has always shown content expertise, emotional intelligence, a willingness to connect, honesty in assessment, and an ego-free launching pad.

I am thrilled Leora is releasing a book of her experiences and expertise that I will always look upon as transformational.

You will read about how to address challenges in a clear and methodical way and learn the tools to continue on the path to greater success personally and professionally. Buy it, you will not regret it.

Kelly Grant
Independent Senior IT Security Specialist

***

I met Leora a couple years ago when I was going through a transition in my career. I had taken early retirement and was reflecting on my life.

Her approach to the interview process revitalized my spirit and helped me to focus on the successes of my career and the fact that I still had significant value to contribute to the industry.

The mining industry is all about people; Leora's great people skills made the interview very exciting. She skillfully and comfortably draws out an individual's strengths and builds focus by helping to make these attributes all of value in approaching the job market.

She takes the time to be thorough and has tremendous listening and comprehension skills. I had 37 years of experiences to share. This one interview experience made me recognize I was not ready to retire.

It is with thanks, honor, and respect that I provide this testimonial for Leora Bach. Taking time to share her experience in her book *Ace Your C-Suite Interview* is a true reflection of her spirit to the people she has met and influenced, and will be of great value to those she will meet as you read her book.

Lloyd E. Metz
Executive Vice President
Ram River Coal Corp.

***

Leora has an eye for exceptional talent and a natural ease of helping to present it in a manner so that all will recognize it. This is a talent in its own right that comes from extensive experience and a dedication rooted in a passion for one's work.

Perhaps it is her possession of that passion that allows her to easily identify it in others.

Many times, as professionals with a lifetime of experience focused on our respective fields, we forget how to sell ourselves, and it is difficult to understand why others may not recognize that we are the best Candidate for a role.

Leora's strength is in guiding skilled Candidates through the process of distilling their talents and bringing them to the surface so that they are readily apparent to a potential employer.

Matt Melnyk
Chief Geologist
Bullion Exploration Inc.

***

Leora helped me recruit high-level executives, including a Corporate CFO and a Vice-President of Business Development, as well as several mining specialists for different managerial functions at our mine site in Panama.

What impressed me most, from the beginning, was Leora's interest in understanding the Company's culture, values, organization, and modus operandi, meeting our people and "walking the site" to truly understand the requirements of a particular job before initiating a search.

From that initial stage, Leora would design a work plan to cover all possible search options (geographic regions, languages, Company cultures) and would diligently execute until several ideal Candidates were identified. Her profiling of each short-listed Candidate was thorough and well-structured, comparatively analyzing weaknesses and strengths in a very objective manner.

The end result of Leora's approach and commitment to each mission consistently exceeded our expectations and helped us build a strong team, from accountants to mine managers.

I have never been on the other side, i.e. a Candidate, but can tell that Leora's *Ace Your C-Suite Interview* is as intelligently structured and helpful as her headhunting expertise.

Joao C. Manuel
Chief Executive Officer
Petaquilla Minerals Ltd

***

I have the absolute honor and privilege to have known Leora firstly as a Candidate after I qualified as a Chartered Accountant in 1991 and then as our exclusive Headhunter from 1992 through to 1995.

Leora was retained by our Company to assist us with a startup where she was personally responsible for hiring in excess of 130 people, across multiple levels of staff in every category of skills – right up to the Executive level.

Initially, this was all under immense pressure while the business got off the ground. There was no room for error. We needed to employ the right people quickly. From my perspective, it was a no brainer to contract with her based on my personal experience. What a star!

Leora was a true mentor to me when I applied for a position in 1991. This was critical to ensure Client and Candidate needs were aligned. She was clear with Client's needs and how to deal with the interview process.

I have known Leora for 24 years, and I still call on her for advice even though we are both living on opposite sides of the globe. This book will no doubt be a best seller!

Richard Biesheuvel
Ex CEO Games Africa (Pty) Ltd
Current Group Executive Project Management Coffey
International Ltd

Table of Contents

Introduction

I wrote this book for you.

If you have ever found yourself in a job that you hated, and could not bear the thought of dragging your body to work for one more day, but did not know where or even how to start looking for another job, then this book is for you.

If you've taken early retirement or been "forced" into it and would give anything to get back into the job market and have just one more shot at a Senior Executive position, then keep reading.

If you feel that you've outlived your usefulness, but deep down inside, you just know that you still have so much to offer, then it is no coincidence that you are reading this book.

If you've ever been downsized or fired from a job that you truly loved, and some benevolent soul gave you this book, consider it a gift.

I understand full well the shock, devastation and emotional toll a job loss of a primary breadwinner has on an entire family.

Please take heart, I have witnessed this hundreds of times and coached more people through this particular event in their lives, than I can remember. All these Candidates were coached in a way that was tailored to their specific needs and circumstances. Without fail, they all found work again and each became very successful.

Even I, was stunned at some of the transformations that I saw, with outcomes of success that even exceeded my wildest expectations.

It's amazing what happens when you see someone rekindle that desire and ambition that lay dormant for so many years, buried under layers of remorse, regret, guilt and often just being constantly undermined and used.

A University Professor of mine taught me the following maxim and I too have used it during my darkest periods. *"It's always too soon to give up; but it's never too late to start!"*

We know that real and lasting change happens from the inside out. I coach my Candidates through their blocks and limiting beliefs by physically showing them how amazing, creative and talented they are; that their leadership is definitely needed, but most importantly, I help them realize how much they *still* have to offer a prospective Employer.

You will read the success stories of other Candidates, learn what to do and what *not* to do and see what you have to do to change your mindset, and make sustainable paradigm shifts.

Interspersed with the stories and "what to do's" - you'll find some cartoons for light relief because we all need to laugh. It diffuses the seriousness of the situation and humor is great for healing!

All names of Candidates in the various stories that you will read have been changed to protect their privacy. In most instances, even the industries in which they worked have been changed to add an additional layer of anonymity.

I have also capitalized certain nouns, such as Candidates, Clients and Coaching Clients for emphasis. Synonyms such as Curriculum Vitae, or simply CV, are used interchangeably with Resume, which is more commonly used in North America.

I use the words Client and Company interchangeably because a Client, from my perspective, is quite simply a Company looking to hire and fill a position.

My personal agenda for writing this book is two-fold:

1. To give people hope, and

2. To guide them through a transformational process to ultimate success.

The stories will inspire you and give you hope. The various "Action Steps", segments at the end of each chapter have deliberately been kept to just three, action steps you have to take. This is by design. I could have given you 10 - 15 things to do, but I found that *"an overwhelmed mind does nothing"* and that's the last thing I want you to do!

I want this book to be an informal and enjoyable read. Transformation is never an easy process; we all know it requires work and often a lot of work. Finding a job is no exception. Early on in my career, a Senior Executive told me that, "Finding a job is a full time job!" - I now know this to be true, but I still wanted to make the process a fun and pleasurable experience.

See your transformation as a journey, a journey on which you are not alone. I will be with you every step of the way, guiding you, mentoring you, and illuminating the way when the road ahead looks dark and the unknown, formidable.

This journey will have a starting point (wherever you are now in your career) and an end goal, a final destination that you know you have reached when you transition to your next position. A position in which you are thriving! Surviving will belong to your distant past - you will never settle for that again.

It's time to start this journey with you in the driver's seat, and me as your co-pilot; a road trip where we'll laugh, and you'll learn a lot while you transform into the person that you knew deep down you always could be. Let's do this!

CHAPTER 1

Why I Wrote This Book

"A wise man can learn more from a foolish question than a fool can learn from a wise answer."

Bruce Lee

From Interviewee To Interviewer

It was the second half of the Academic year, and like me, many of the students in my class were frenetically preparing to meet with several Professional Services Firms to find employment as Articled Clerks, a compulsory requirement to become a Chartered Accountant (The equivalent of a Certified Public Accountant (CPA) in North America).

I was studying for my Bachelor of Commerce degree at the University of Cape Town in South Africa, and becoming articled was the next step in the process.

Before classes started, during breaks, and at the end of the school day, we all excitedly discussed amongst ourselves how the process was going, which were the good firms and who had great interviews etc.-but no-one had ever given me advice on interviewing, which I now think should be part of every curriculum. I never even heard anyone discuss it, or for that matter, how to prepare and more specifically, what to do or say in an interview; there was simply no guidance whatsoever.

So, I relied on my innate instinct to dress properly, smile, be engaging, have a Resume prepared, be all set to answer questions honestly and appear interested.

I made a list of the firms I liked and proceeded to arrange interviews on my free afternoons.

My approach was to find out about the firms, see what my friends thought of them and even try and see if I knew any "insiders" who could perhaps provide some additional information. It's always good to have an inside contact, right?

I also knew that I had to present myself as the professional person that I hoped to become. Beyond that, I was articulate, energetic and enthusiastic to commence my career.

What more could anyone expect from me? After all, I was only 22 years old and this was my first permanent position.

For the most part, my strategy, such as it was, worked really well. I'd already had three or four good interviews behind me where the people that I had met with, were really nice. The questions were typically the same and what I expected - so no surprises there.

The Staff Partners interviewing me were interested in my background, family history, why I was interested in the Profession, my University Grades, etc.- simple, easy, innocuous questions to answer. So, I had no reason to expect anything different; however, the next interview was *very* different…

I showed up with the same perky enthusiasm as I had done before, with all my previous interviews. It was a small to medium-sized firm and I was met by a young Partner who informed me that we would be joined by another Partner and I would be interviewed by both of them.

He led me into a small meeting room and we were joined shortly thereafter by the aforementioned gentleman, another fairly young

Partner. They were both really nice and I liked them immediately. The interview was proceeding perfectly when suddenly the door was flung open and "Dinosaurus Interruptus" emerged.

"Did you guys get tickets to the movie yet?" he bellowed, not seeming to mind his own intrusion.

The one Partner looked annoyed and said, "Peter, we're in a meeting!"

Ignoring the Partner who had just spoken, he continued unabashed, "Well! Did you guys manage to get tickets?"

The two nice Partners exchanged glances with one another and then the second one spoke up and said firmly, "Can't you see we are busy interviewing?!"

"Oh," said Peter, "why don't I join you then?"

My heart sank; I had a feeling in the depth of my gut that this was not going to be good.

The other two Partners looked at each other; no-one invited him in or said a word - but Peter needed no invitation. This bull just sallied forth.

He pulled out a chair and sat down at this now, clearly, over-crowded small table. What a jerk, I thought. The atmosphere in the room changed immediately and the other two Partners were clearly uncomfortable.

Then, as if noticing me for the first time, he turned to bestow his undivided attention on me. "Well," he said, "Where do you see yourself in five years' time?" I froze. I was still trying to come to terms with this cad kiboshing my interview!

He repeated the question more sternly with a formidable gaze that was boring holes into me. My mind was simply a blank; I knew I had to answer his question, but in this moment, I could not come up with anything remotely appropriate or eloquent enough to satisfy him. It was excruciating.

After what seemed like an indeterminable amount of time, with me still in shocked silence and he staring aggressively, I was finally put out of my misery. Leaning in, he growled sarcastically, "I'll tell you where you'll be in five years' time! - You'll be five years older!" And with that, he leaned back in his chair and roared with laughter at the sheer brilliance of his own joke.

No-one else laughed or said a word. I was embarrassed and humiliated. After a few seconds, I turned to the other two Partners and thanked them for seeing me and quietly exited the room and the firm without ever looking back.

It was a horrible interview, in fact, the worst I have ever had - but it was a game changer. I knew from that day forward that I would *never* leave anything to chance again and I never have; and doing just that *one* thing has made ALL the difference to my life!

When I was alone, I reflected on that interview and replayed the event over and over again in my mind. I guess it was my way of doing a post mortem. I was so ashamed; I never discussed it with anyone, not even my family - but one thing I knew for sure was that, this experience had taught me an irrefutable truth - I was entirely 100% responsible for what happened to me!

What exactly do I mean by that? I realized it was *my* responsibility to take control of *my* future; no longer could I expect that my employer would determine my future and that with at least my first job; I could coast, see what I liked and then decide what I would do with the rest of my life.

Up until then, I just thought life would take care of itself and as time progressed, I would have a natural inclination to guide my career in a direction towards the activities that I loved and away from those that did not interest me. In my naiveté, I honestly believed that someone would come along with a great opportunity and offer it to me. It never occurred to me that *I* needed to have a well thought out plan for *my* life; something specific with congruent goals that I was working towards.

That was one thing that I realized, but not the only thing; I also learned that I could *never* underestimate what the other person might know or ask me. In other words, I had to be prepared for anything!

"Where do I see myself in 15 years? I wish you wouldn't ask that!"

Fortunately, I did find a Firm that I really liked and Articled with them. After four years, I went back to university to commence my second degree. During that time, I gave in to my "wanderlust" to explore bigger opportunities; this took me to Johannesburg, where I worked for another Professional Services Firm.

After two years with them, I had a great interview with one of the top Executive Search Firms in Johannesburg, and to my surprise, I got a call from them shortly after my interview, not for a position with one of their Clients, but for an opportunity to work directly with them. An opportunity that really *did* change the direction of my career - in a wonderful way!

A few years later, when I felt that I had learned enough to go on my own; I decided to start my own Executive Search Firm, which became one of the Premier Boutique Firms in the city. As Johannesburg is the largest city in South Africa, it was also head office to most companies, especially the Mining Conglomerates and Finance Houses amongst others, most of whom were my Clients.

It was quite simply an amazing time in my life. I loved what I did; I loved the Clients that I headhunted for and the Candidates that I interviewed.

I was learning so much about running a business, but I was restless because there was still *one* specific goal that I *really* wanted. North American experience!

In the mid-1990s, I immigrated to Canada and joined one of the Big Four Professional Services Firms in Vancouver, British Columbia. I was a Senior Manager on the Consulting side within the Executive Search Division until The Securities and Exchange Commission (SEC) ruled that it was a conflict of interest for Professional Service Firms to offer Executive Search as a service to their Clients.

So, within a year of this ruling, we were sold, and our group became a subsidiary of one of the biggest Executive Search Firms in the world; however, culturally it was not a good fit for me and most of my erstwhile colleagues. Eventually, most of us left to pursue other interests or start our own firms.

In 2010, I immigrated once again - to the United States, where I currently reside. I absolutely love it here and know this is where I am meant to be!

What I have discovered, having lived and worked in three separate countries, is that no matter where in the world you are, people are still the same and we all basically want the same things.

Beyond Maslow's theory of hierarchical needs, once one's basic needs are met, all people want to be able to provide a wonderful life for their families. In order to do that, they need to satisfy a certain level of income, in order to satisfy a certain level of income, they need a great job, and in order to get a great job, they need some incredible help preparing them to Ace an Interview! That's where I come in.

Lifting The Corporate Veil

I have been a Headhunter for over 25 years, and have interviewed more than 20,000 people in that time period. My Client and Candidate bases are both global.

I have literally worked with and interviewed people from all four corners of the world, which has kept the work interesting and filled with variety. This diversity amongst my Candidate base has filled me with intrigue and those ever gnawing questions: What makes people tick? Why do they do the things they do? How do I best serve and help them realize *their* dreams?

I work exclusively on a retained Executive Search basis, which means that most of my time and resources are directed towards working with a Client to head-hunt the exact person or people that, that Company is looking for.

In Chapter 4, I will cover the difference between Contingency Recruiting and Retained Executive Search in detail and how it directly affects a Candidate; for now - I just want to mention that most of the people that I interview are gainfully employed and it is my job to lure them away from where they currently work and what they have, to a more exciting opportunity with my Client.

The point being, if someone is head-hunted, goes through an Executive Search Process and still doesn't get the position, at worst, they might be disappointed; however, as they are already employed, they are not affected adversely or compromised financially by the experience.

However, when there is a recession in a certain niche market or the economy as a whole, then my inbox is full with unsolicited Resumes from Candidates who desperately need work because their very livelihood depends on it.

I hate it when this happens and my feelings for anyone in this situation are absolutely heartfelt. In fact, it is one of the main reasons why I wrote this book.

During recessionary times, jobs are few and the competition fiercer than ever - which means that in order for a Candidate to stand a better than average chance of getting a position, they need to be able to stand out from the crowd and be substantially better; sadly, most people don't have a clue how to do this, through no fault of their own.

I cannot even remember how many Senior Executives I have interviewed who, after losing their jobs, are still in a deep state of shock and quietly mumbled to me, "I just didn't see this coming... I've been with the Company for over twenty years." I cannot tell you how heartbreaking it is to hear and how badly, I'm affected by it - it literally keeps me up at night.

So, I decided to write this book and educate my Candidates about what happens behind the scenes, "Lifting the Corporate Veil" as it were, to teach them:

- How Company Executives make hiring decisions

- How our industry works - I'm referring to working with Head-hunters, Recruiting Agencies, Human Resource Professionals and how we all differ and how that difference directly affects the Candidates

- How they need to differentiate themselves from every other Candidate on the short-list

- How to ultimately change their mindset, behavior and thinking to be able to handle *any* question posed to them in an interview, rather than "parroting" silly clichéd answers like a monkey!

How To Get The Most Benefit Out Of This Book

I have spent decades coaching my short-list Candidates and my private Clients who are Job Seekers, pursuing either a specific opportunity or needing to replace a senior position recently lost.

I have used strategies and tips with my Candidates and Clients that I have honed, crafted and refined over the years with immense success.

You will read the story of a Candidate who was a rank outsider on a Search Assignment, (conducted by a firm other than my own) approach me for help to coach him through the process. By reframing and repositioning him, by highlighting his unique strengths (and yes - you have them too!) won a seven figure salary over his competition.

You will hear a story of one of my private Coaching Clients who had been out of work for a year or longer, whose limiting beliefs I turned around. And, after working with me for four months, received three confirmed job offers, all in the high six figure range.

This is what I love to do most - help people who have lost all hope and given up on themselves; show them that they can turn their situations around and be better off than before, and better off still than they ever imagined!

This book was written for all people in the C-Suite, and those that aren't yet there, but certainly aspire to be. Honestly, anyone with ambition to better their station in life will learn from the principles and guidance in this book.

I resolved to write this book exclusively for Candidates because, just like death and taxes, the one thing in life you can be sure of is that at some stage in your career, you *will* be a Candidate interviewing for a position - so you may as well be prepared to best advantage!

I will teach you how Companies evaluate *you,* the Candidate and what they are really looking for. We will turn paradigms upside down and look at life completely differently - that's what you have to do to distinguish yourself because if you do the same standard stuff that everyone else does, you will not be seen as different and certainly never as "special."

All companies want that "incredible talent" that is so elusive and scarce, that they will pay a premium for it!

Now, I can hear you say, "That's not me, I'm not special or an incredible talent, I'm just an ordinary person looking for a job." Trust me, I've interviewed over twenty thousand people and not a single person was the same! They were all different and those differences made *all* the difference - it's what makes everyone unique.

From your genes, to your upbringing, to the specific talents that you have, your education, industry experience, skill set, management style and leadership skills (to name a few) make you far from ordinary and very special indeed - you just don't know how to showcase those attributes yet, but in time you will.

I will be with you on this transformational journey, every step of the way. I will explain what I do, why I do it, and the specific logic behind this approach.

You will learn how to reposition yourself as "the best Candidate for the job", and you will use your new won confidence to expertly and professionally explain to your Interviewer, or interview Panel, why you *are* the best person for the role and why they definitely *need* to hire you, without even mentioning *that* they need to hire you.

They will be so engaged in what you are saying that their immediate reaction, once you've left the room, will be - "We have to get this person on board before someone else hires them!"

Trust me, I know this for a fact because, as the Executive Search Consultant, I'm a facilitator on the Panel interviews that my Senior Executives have, so I'm in the room when these conversations take place.

The bad news is that this kind of transformation is not guaranteed. It only happens when you do the work. Yes, that's right! Success takes work, but the good news is - you only have to put in the effort to reposition and re-frame yourself once and the rate of return on that investment, you'll enjoy in perpetuity.

Additional benefits to doing this are that you will learn so much about yourself, and what you learn will be applicable to many different areas of your life.

Your confidence and self-esteem will grow and help you to negotiate better in both your work and personal relationships. It will improve your bargaining position to help you get what you want. This will all happen seamlessly without you even noticing it once you really *know* who you are and *what* you have to offer.

My sincere desire for you is to see you move from surviving in a position to thriving in a role within a Company that respects and values *who* you are and *what* you have to contribute!

Now, to reap the kind of benefits that you will read about in the stories from my private Coaching Clients, you will have your work cut out for you. My Coaching Clients work really hard.

Those who do everything I tell them to do - are rewarded with either a specific opportunity that they wanted or several job offers beyond what they hoped for or expected. The caveat is you *have* to do the exercises. You will *not* be successful just by reading the book!

Action Steps

1. Read the book through thoroughly once.

2. Read the book again. This time, underline, make notations, do whatever you need to do to easily find certain sections that you want to come back to.

3. Do the exercises - this is the action that you absolutely need to take to see the results that you want.

CHAPTER 2

Mindset, Paradigms And Limiting Beliefs

"Rule Your Mind, Or It Will Rule You."

Horace

From Victim To Victor

I received a call from Henry in February 2011 and he asked me if I would meet with him. He had lost his job a year earlier when the industry he worked in was hit by a recession. The Company had downsized several of their Executives and Senior Professionals. Unfortunately, Henry ended up being one of them.

Henry was a six figure earner and the Company he worked for was kind enough to offer him one year's severance, which he had almost entirely consumed by the time he called me.

I invited Henry for lunch because I wanted to meet in a more informal, and relaxed setting than my office. Now, although we had spoken to each other over the phone and traded emails, we had never yet met in person, so I had no idea what he looked like or what to expect.

I arrived early and while sitting at our table, I watched the patrons arrive for lunch, curious as to which one Henry would be. Suddenly, a gentleman in a light grey suit came over to me. I realized immediately that he recognized me from my profile picture on my website.

He was nicely dressed, articulate, very professional in his demeanor, engaging and friendly. Henry stuck his hand out to greet me, "Hello," he said warmly, "thank you for seeing me!"

"You're very welcome," I said, wondering why there would be *any* reason for him not being able to find work. And then he gave me one.

"You are the only Headhunter in this city who has the decency to return my calls. Thank you so much for seeing me!" he reiterated.

"Why is that?" I asked.

"I'm too old," said Henry, "I know that my age is counting against me and because of that I can't find a job! I'm just so desperate. Do you think that I *can* find a job?" he asked me sincerely.

"Of course," I said, "Companies don't hire based on age; they hire based on competence, skills, education and experience, and *all* that, you *do* have to offer!"

We spoke for a long time. After lunch, I went through his Resume in great detail. Fortunately, we were in a booth and this afforded us a substantial amount of much needed privacy.

I also wanted Henry to just talk… about everything and anything...his frustrations, fears, disappointments, simply anything at all. I just wanted him to get it all out and off his chest so that I could see where his head was at, and what he feared the most.

I needed to know not just that my work was cut out for me, but where I needed to start with him.

Henry was well educated; he had an undergraduate degree in Engineering (specific to his industry) and a Masters in Economics.

His track record was stable and his career included several senior positions with large companies within his industry.

After listening to him for over two hours, it was clear that the biggest obstacle preventing Henry from getting another position was his limiting belief that he was too old. Casual reassurance on my part that he had nothing to worry about and that it was just a matter of waiting for the right opportunity to come along was *not* going to cut it!

He really needed help. So, I offered to coach Henry until he found a position, and not just *any* position, but one that would meet *all* his expectations.

I approached all my coaching from the perspective that he *was* the best person for the job. We would dig up dozens of reasons to justify this position, always substantiated by his excellent education, past track record of success, his specific skills, and the extensive experience that he had within his industry.

We NEVER once spoke about age. I never ever asked him his age and I had no interest whatsoever in finding out. I wanted him to not even think about it - so I changed his focus to everything he was more than capable of doing....

I convinced him over and over again, until it was inculcated into his mind that he *was* the best Candidate for the job - because he could contribute immediately!

And what Company would *not* want to hire someone who could contribute immediately to whatever they needed most?

We met a few more times in person. Sometimes, he would come to my office and other times we would speak on the phone. I gave him several assignments to do and after a few weeks, I noticed that he looked different. He was more assertive, and certainly more confident.

Even his gait had changed. He walked erectly, where previously he had a slight slouch; Henry was also more purposeful in stating what he wanted from the next prospective employer. He was also more sure of what he specifically wanted to do.

Now remember, at the beginning of this story, I had mentioned that Henry had initially called me in February 2011.

Well in June 2011 (yes! - we're talking a mere four months later), I received an email from Henry and I quote, "I am in the middle of decision making mode. Things have happened so fast over the last three weeks; I now have the following…" and he began to describe in detail three confirmed job offers in writing, all of which were excellent opportunities at a much higher level of compensation than he had ever earned before!

Now to be fair, Henry worked really hard, he did every assignment that I asked of him, he never resisted and he never balked at my suggestion to do anything that involved working towards finding the next opportunity.

I was so impressed and really proud of him, and of course, reassured that what I had always believed was true. Limiting beliefs are just that - limiting. They don't serve us in any way; they just hold us back and paralyze us in fear…

Finally just to tie up loose ends in this story, Henry sent me a testimonial, but for personal reasons did not want his name mentioned. So to respect his wishes, I will share with you what he wrote, anonymously.

"When I met Leora, my self-confidence had taken a big hit. Not only did I have no job prospects, but I was at a loss as to how to rekindle the motivation for a successful job search.

From the moment we met, she focused my confidence and belief system on the benefits that I could offer to any potential employer.

Over a 4 month period, Leora never failed to impress on me the potential that I had, based on my experience and track record - in short, she coached me in how I could approach any job opportunity in the knowledge that I was the best Candidate for the job.

My positive attitude opened doors for me, leading to no less than 3 job offers!"

One final word on this story; what worked for Henry works for everyone who applies the system. What I cannot guarantee is the length of time it will take because there are so many factors that can influence the process. However, with most of the people that I have worked with, the time frame has usually been around three to four months.

What I can guarantee is that you will get better and better, and be more than ready when the right opportunity presents itself. Isn't that the definition of luck? When preparation meets opportunity!

© Randy Glasbergen
www.glasbergen.com

"Don't think of me as a 54 year old job applicant.
Think of it as getting two 27 year olds for the price of one!"

Mindset, Paradigms And Limiting Beliefs

What Are They And How Do They Hold Us Back?

A Mindset is a fixed mental attitude that predisposes a person's responses to and interpretations of, situations.

So, someone's mindset will determine how they think, what they believe is true, and how they behave, and react to situations that happen to them.

When researching this topic, I learned that there were basically two kinds of mindsets.

1. **Growth Mindsets: Primarily possessed by positive people, who:**

   - Were open-minded and keen to learn new things
   - Believed that failure was actually an opportunity in disguise because you could learn from it
   - Embraced change and welcomed challenges
   - Knew how to capitalize on their strengths, and
   - Were prepared to work on their weaknesses

2. **Fixed Mindsets: Primarily possessed by negative people, who:**

   - Conversely did not deal well with change, and new challenges
   - Felt victimized by their circumstances
   - Believed their abilities were limited and felt that they were not dealt a "fair hand of cards" at birth
   - Avoided anything that might have the slightest risk of failure or would take them out of their comfort zone
   - Most often than not responded to questions, challenges, requests and suggestions with that customary, paralyzing catchphrase, "I can't!"

Paradigms are a collection of false beliefs embedded in your subconscious mind. They are the product of years and years of conditioning. Included in this collection is that "little naysayer" that keeps you safe by keeping you stuck.

That inner voice that sabotages and stamps out your brilliant, bold ideas that would advance your life and career, by reassuring you that if you ventured forward and took that risk, you would *fail*, so it's better to not even contemplate doing it.

Limiting Beliefs are things that we believe to be true, but sadly often those beliefs are based on our own interpretation of painful, past experiences. Beliefs can also be handed down by our parents, based on their past experiences; but irrespective of where limiting beliefs come from, these beliefs all have a common denominator - They hold us back.

How To Break Through These Barriers And Strangleholds

I am not a Psychologist, nor am I an actor that plays one on TV - so when researching the topic of Mindset, Paradigms and Limiting Beliefs; the definitions seemed to be so similar to me that one can really get caught up in the semantics of each.

After a while, I realized that if I'm finding this confusing, other people will as well. Eventually, it all sounded like a tangled ball of "knotty nonsense" that we store in our subconscious mind.

These thoughts are inevitably negative thoughts that keep us captive, and create a stranglehold on the positive things we need to say to ourselves; the behaviors that we need to embrace, and the action that we need to take to move us forward.

For the sake of simplicity, you have a Conscious Mind and a Subconscious Mind. The Conscious Mind governs your logic and decision making processes.

If you decide to block some time off, to update your Profile on LinkedIn for example, that is a conscious decision that you have just made. It does not require a specific belief or paradigm shift - it is simply a decision that you have made to carry out a specific task.

On the other hand, the Subconscious Mind is far more complex. This part of your mind controls all your involuntary functions, such as your heart beating. Imagine if you had to try to control your own heart beat? That would be insanely difficult!

It is also the place where our memories and beliefs are stored, and as you now know, a lot of our beliefs are formed based on bad past experiences or inherited fears that have been passed down.

The Subconscious Mind is that part of our mind that runs on autopilot - that wants to protect us all the time from perceived (not necessary real) threats in our environment. It wants to protect us from danger, and how does it do this? - with that small, inner little voice that tells you *not* to do certain things (which at times really *is* a good thing) but most of the time, it stops you from doing the *very* thing that you need to do!

However, the good news is we can, with concerted effort, override the Subconscious Mind by choosing to take specific action that is in strong contrast to the limiting beliefs we hold.

I know at this point, you're probably thinking, "Easier said than done!" and you would be right - but do you want to be right or do you want to be successful?

So How Do We Actually Do This?

1. First, slow down and become an "observer" to your thoughts. Don't try and control your thoughts, just see what comes up, and make a note of them - write them down. Often, thoughts are difficult to identify as a specific thought, so be vigilant as to how certain things make you *feel*.

   See which experiences and memories are triggers for you. For example, if you have recently lost your job - list all the feelings attached to how you felt about that happening. Your shock, anger, resentment about the unfairness of it all - list all those feelings...Also list your limiting beliefs.

   Change always happens from the inside out. You also cannot change what you don't admit to - and to admit to something, you have to give credence to its existence. You do this by writing it down and looking at it.

   Now don't be lazy - this is about doing something good and constructive for you. Make that list as long as possible, and every time a new thought comes up associated with that event, add it to your list. Add additional limiting beliefs as they come to mind.

2. Then look at that list, once you are satisfied that there isn't another thing that you could possibly add, rest easy that for now, it's as complete as you need it to be.

   Allow yourself to "mourn" the loss of that position, feel resentment, anger, whatever it is - don't hold back.

   Give yourself as much time as you need (I'm talking about days and at most a few weeks, not months or years - we have work to do, and no matter what you think right now, your best days are still ahead!)

3. When you are ready to move on, make another list and write down all the reasons why you deserve to have a position.

   Take your list of limiting beliefs, and fears and rewrite them in the positive. Write down the complete opposite of every fear and limiting belief you have; for example:

Limiting Belief/Fear:

I'll never get another job, my best years are behind me, the market is too competitive; companies only want younger people.

New Positive Belief:

I have so much to offer a prospective employer; I'm highly skilled and I have extensive experience in my industry.

There is no substitute for experience. Any company that hired me would be fortunate to have me; my learning curve is short because I can contribute immediately! Companies are always hiring, and there are companies looking for my skills and experience right now!

Now focus ONLY on the reframed positive beliefs.

Throw the negative lists away - you will never need them again. Look for past successes to substantiate the reframed positive statements you have written down. Go over this a few times a day. You *have* to get into the mindset that you absolutely *can* and *will* find work again!

Action Steps

1. Acknowledge what has happened to you. You cannot deal with it if you keep it a secret. Speak to your family, friends and trusted advisors - the people who love and support you. You are not the first person to lose a job - speak to former colleagues and friends whom you respect, and who you know of that went through the same experience - ask them how they felt, and how they ultimately turned things around. It always feels better to know that you are not alone.

2. List your worst fears; ask yourself if these are *really* true statements. Inevitably, they are not. Find logical reasons to confirm that these negative statements are definitely *not* true. Remember, if you previously had a position and a good track record, you are *better* now. You have more experience, and you've solved more problems for your Company.

3. Go over your list of reframed positive statements until they are inculcated into your mind and your new belief is that you absolutely *will* come back to the work force better and stronger than before!

   Now I have to say this one last thing: If you are committed to changing the way you think, speak and behave, and most importantly, are doing what I ask of you - you *absolutely* will have another job offer, if not several - because you will be doing things you've never done before, and you will be presenting yourself to the outside world, and prospective employers in a completely different way.

CHAPTER 3

Why Having A Strategy
Is Absolutely Critical

*"I believe that people make their own luck by
great preparation and good strategy."*

Jack Canfield

From Game Plan To Game Changer

It was just after the financial crisis of 2008, considered by many
leading economists to have been the worst financial crisis since
the Great Depression of the 1930s. I remember one awful and
particularly grim day at the end of September 2008, when the Dow
fell 777 points in just one day! The next day, Stock Markets all
over the globe were down as the world watched in horror to see
what would happen next.

My mind was not on work; I was on the Internet almost all day
watching the hourly breaking news. I wanted to know how this
was going to affect my Clients.

I remembered a few months earlier in April, speaking to a Client
of mine, a Chief Operating Officer, about whether he "felt"
something was different - did *he* feel the market was changing? I
enquired, because I certainly did. Well, he didn't and reassured me

that all was well, and their Company was carrying on with their planned expansion.

I remember asking several other Clients and close friends, all of whom worked at the C-Suite level, if they felt that the market was over-heated. Every single one of them assured me that everything was fine and that the economy, especially in North America, was in really good shape. I had nothing to worry about.

Now with hindsight we all know, that was not the case. In fact, it could not have been further from the truth, but I did not care that my gut feeling was right, I just wanted everything to be better, and for the recovery that follows every recession to start immediately. I just wanted everything to be "fixed" because in my world, during contracting economic times, my Clients shed people, they don't hire!

While still reeling from what had happened, I got a call from one of my CEO Clients. It was the end of November 2008, and he wanted to meet me for lunch. I could not think why he possibly wanted to see me; I knew his Company would certainly not be hiring now.

I met Benson at a restaurant that was mutually convenient for both of us. After a few minutes of pleasantries, he came straight to the point. He had been approached by one of the Biggest Search Firms for a position with one of *their* Clients, and he wanted me to help him get the position.

"I *really* want this job," he said firmly, "and I know you're the best - so I want you to coach me through the process." I wasn't flattered, I was apprehensive. There are so many things that I do *before* I take on a Client.

My position, compared to the access I normally have, would be severely compromised. In fact, I would not have *any* access to the Client at all.

This was not *my* Client and furthermore, Benson was probably not the ideal Candidate for the position. Well, that's what it looked like at first glance, and no one would blame me for making that call; he had absolutely no experience in this particular industry.

Benson was, however, not deterred; he did not see his complete lack of industry experience as a problem. He was determined, and had simply made up his mind that he wanted the job and that was that! The ball was served deftly back into my court…What was I going to do? I could have said, "No," but I liked him and wanted to help.

At least if Benson did *not* get the job, I would be able to say that I tried to get him short-listed. That would have been quite an achievement given his restrictions, and the competition that I knew he would be up against.

But a win over his competition would need a serious strategy and an excellent game plan!

I decided on the following Strategy:

1. Find out everything about the Company
   - Who owned the Company
   - Who founded or started the Company
   - What they did
   - What industry were they in
   - Who was their competition etc.?
   - Were they Public or Private

2. Find out everything about the position
   - Title
   - Duties and Responsibilities of the Role
   - Ideal Candidate Profile

The Game Plan was as follows:

As it was not my Client and Benson had not met with any of the Senior Executives of the Company yet, it was difficult to find out about the Corporate Culture - the most important aspect of *any* job - which you will learn about later on.

So, I asked him to find out as much as he could about the Company Culture, the other Candidates that he was competing against, and generally as much information as he could glean from the Headhunter that had approached him about the opportunity.

He was highly motivated and had done a fine job of gathering the information that I asked of him. However, I was still struggling with how to get past his lack of industry experience.

To compound matters, Benson told me that he had found out that the other Candidates all had the desired industry experience, and one of those Candidates was the CEO of the biggest Company in that particular industry - so he was contending with the stiffest competition imaginable!

I knew that the answer to finding a way to radically distinguish him from the other Candidates lay in going over Benson's background with a "fine tooth comb." I also needed to know as much as I could about the Company - which he informed me was privately owned and had just been bought out by a Venture Capital Firm, and it was *their* decision to hire a new CEO.

Bingo! - That's it, I thought! I can see a way to turn this situation completely around. How convenient to have an Auditing and Consulting background. I decided on the following:

- We would not be competing on Benson's industry strength and expertise because we couldn't, so we did not even mention that at all.

- I told him that he would be best positioned as having excellent business acumen, a visionary with outstanding leadership skills.

- I told him that it was a distinct advantage for us that the Company had been bought out by a Venture Capital Firm because I understood what would be important to *them.*

- As business people, the Partners in the Firm would be looking for a very strong leader with the ability to take the Company to the next level; someone who was a visionary and who could inspire people, and motivate them to want to work with him.

Now I knew Benson well, because he was a Client of mine, and I had headhunted for him before when he was looking for a Vice President. I had seen how well he treated his staff. He was a kind, thoughtful, caring and also charismatic man.

He was a very good businessman, an excellent negotiator and was well respected by his peers.

These were not things Benson had to work at - it was evident in everything he did, including his bearing.

So, we played up his strengths to the degree; that, what he did *not* have would be minimized to the extent that it was barely an issue at all.

I also told Benson that at the CEO level, "soft skills" such as the ones he had, are essential, but technical skills could always be hired to supplement what he did not have in industry experience.

BUT: There was one more thing that still worried me and I had to be convinced beyond a shadow of a doubt that he would be able to position himself as having superior business skills compared to the other Candidates.

Now Benson was currently working for a Public Company, and the position that he wanted, was with a Private Company, so I wanted him to ask whether he could have access to the new Company's financial statements.

He was really uneasy about this and told me that I would make him look like a jerk. "Absolutely not!" I said, "On the contrary, you will look like the Candidate with the best business acumen!"

27

I explained to him that an Executive who was thinking strategically would *never* leave a Company to go to another, without knowing what the financial stability of *that* Company was. He simply *had* to ask!

Benson understood the logic, but was really uncomfortable with the task. I further explained to him that he would probably be the *only* Candidate that had the fortitude to ask. He reluctantly agreed to do so.

Now at the beginning of the process, he told me that there had been five Candidates in the running for this position, including himself. Over the following weeks, the list was culled to three, and then there were two - he was still in the race…Then at the final interview, Benson plucked up the courage to ask.

I asked him afterwards, when he was giving me feedback, what the reaction was because I knew that the Executive Search Committee who was interviewing was *not* obligated to divulge that information. Benson said they looked at him with stunned silence - but did ultimately make the information available to him.

When he discussed this with me, he still seemed so unsure that he had done the right thing, but I was determined that he present himself as the most sagacious Candidate.

A week or two of waiting followed; Benson was on the phone with me daily asking what was taking so long. I reassured him that the reputable firms all did thorough references and pre-employment checks. I knew the wait must have been agonizing, but then the call came…

Benson got the job!

That, my dear "C-Suiters," is how you Ace an Interview!

Shifting The Paradigm From Getting To Giving...

What Most Candidates Do

The overwhelming majority of Candidates present themselves all in the same way. They introduce themselves via a Cover Letter with an accompanying Resume. The content of the Cover Letter usually covers a brief introduction of themselves and then segues into what they have done, where they worked, etc. Then comes what *they* want in terms of the next prospective position and salary package, the part that is *most* important to a Candidate.

Now, we've all heard the famous expression by Theodore Roosevelt, *"No one cares how much you know, until they know how much you care."*

As a Facilitator on the Executive Search Panel (sometimes also referred to as an Executive Search Committee), I have sat in on more Senior Executive level interviews than I can remember, and as a member of the Panel, I've had the advantage of seeing and hearing what Clients *really* think of the Candidates.

I can tell you first hand, no Client in any country in which I have headhunted has ever said I think we should hire this Candidate because he really *needs* the job or that Candidate because he came in as the most *reasonably priced* Candidate.
No, that never happens!

The Executive Search Panel interviews from *their* perspective. So, if you really want another position or if you are simply changing from one position to another, the first thing you absolutely need to get into your head is - it's not about what you want! As Theodore Roosevelt so wisely said, they really don't care about you!

The Executive Search Panel, who serves the interests of the Company as a whole, is interested in only one thing - What you can do for *them*! This same rule applies if you are being interviewed individually by one or several Senior Managers and Executives over a period of weeks.

In other words - you have to shift your paradigm from getting to giving. You need to consider what is *most important* to *them.*

What All Candidates *Should* Do

So, the bottom line is you have to change the way you think and approach your next job search.

I cannot recommend strongly enough that you keep this thought uppermost in your mind when you are drawing up that Cover Letter, Resume, and definitely throughout the Interview Process.

I would add further that you should also be thinking of what you have to offer when you are presenting yourself on Social Media; this is your first introduction to the world, and ultimately future Employer.

In fact, a completely authentic paradigm shift in your thinking (once you've understood the concept and seen the light!) should follow through, not just until you have the position - but should be a cue for you to seriously re-evaluate the way you manage and lead your staff.

What Clients *Really* Want

Most companies hire to fill critical positions if they are new, and are growing organically at a rapid pace or replace key roles that have recently become vacant because the current incumbent has resigned and moved on. Again, there are other situations where the existing incumbent has not met the Company's expectations and may have been asked to leave the Company.

Whatever the reason, the Company will have very high expectations of the *incoming incumbent,* and that might be *you* - so we have to talk about this...

- If the Company is a start-up and the position is newly created, you may well have more leeway than usual, and the opportunity to set up the department or lead the Company as you see fit.

  However even in this situation, depending on your level of seniority, there will always be someone that you need to get approval from - either a Senior Executive (Superior); perhaps even more than one person will have input in how you set up and run a department.

If your position is that of CEO - you will need the Board of Director's approval for most critical decisions that have serious impact and consequences for the Company. For decisions of lesser importance, you will have more latitude.

- If the position you are filling was vacated by someone else - you will have a bigger upward climb. That person may have been very good at what they did and now the people that you will report to (either a direct Superior or the Board of Directors) will be looking to see if you match up at the very least.

- Finally there is a third option; if the previous incumbent did *not* meet their expectations, then you have the *most* serious challenge to overcome because now your burden is not only to be able to convince them that you are up to the task, and more than competent to take on the role, but you also have to worry about restoring their trust and faith!

They will be more than skeptical of anyone coming in, and you will really have to bring your "A-Game" to the table to thwart their fears and convince them, that they have nothing to be concerned about.

The reason for the position being vacant will not change *what* the Company wants, but knowing *why* a position is vacant may well affect *your* approach to how you position yourself.

Basically every Client wants the following:

- Someone who can take their "pain" away and that might simply be a Senior Manager, Professional person, or an Executive who can do things so efficiently that they don't have to worry about what that person does.

By saying that the Client does "not have to worry about what that person does" - I mean that the Company hiring the individual wants someone so competent that they don't have to micromanage that person. The Company should be able to have implicit trust in that person's competency.

- A Candidate whose honesty and integrity is beyond reproach.

- A Person who is the consummate team-player; who has a strong network of contacts, and can deal with people at all levels. Someone perfectly capable of, and comfortable with, dealing with key Stakeholders like The Board of Directors, Bankers, External Auditors, Governmental Authorities, Investment Bankers etc.

- Someone who their colleagues respect, admire and like working with.

- An Executive who can meet challenges with grace and fortitude - someone who subordinates look up to, all people want to work with, and in whom the Board of Directors has implicit confidence and trust.

- A Leader who commands (not demands) respect by having earned it based on the goals they set and achieve, the way they behave and most importantly, how they treat people!

"You married *me* — that proves you're brilliant and a great judge of character. Put that on your résumé!"

You Are Your Most Important Project

"Be yourself, everyone else is already taken" - Oscar Wilde. Ever heard this expression? You may wonder why this is so important.

Aren't we told as children to be more like "so and so"? Then our "well-meaning" parents and most especially teachers pointed out to us how much better "so and so "was at everything we were not. "Well-meaning" because for most adults, they believe that denigrating a child "just a little" will serve as enormous motivation.

Well, it never worked on me! I always felt insulted because even as a child I felt that my other talents were being ignored. I already knew that I was different, but I wanted to be loved, respected and admired for those differences - not compared to someone else for an attribute that *they* possessed, which wasn't even important to me.

Comparisons are odious. What's even worse is that this kind of affront is not limited to when we are growing up. We enter the corporate world as young adults and often well into our careers; many of us will end up working for bosses who do the same.

They will play us off against our peers and colleagues, but the difference is when it is done in adulthood in a corporate setting, the denigration is not well-meaning, it is meant to hurt and humiliate.

I have interviewed so many senior professionals whose immediate superiors were so abusive that these Candidates were on the verge of a nervous breakdown. I have interviewed even more Candidates who sat in front of me, and told me what happened "behind closed doors" and how, even in the face of continuous and escalating abuse, they had still not "broken down" - so their bosses got rid of them by firing them in a spectacularly degrading way.

They sit in front of me wondering what they did wrong or worse, wondering what they did to deserve this. No-one deserves this and it's devastating to hear these stories, but the good news is, every day is another chance for a new beginning.

A chance to take your Power back! And how, do you take your Power back? Well, I'm about to tell you exactly how…

Now, some of you might sadly have had an experience such as I've described; most of you have probably not. You may just be changing jobs, and have been downsized in a very caring and respectful manner, or you may simply have been approached by a Headhunter or Senior HR person at a Company and wish to prepare yourself to best advantage for the interviews that will be coming up.

Whatever your reason for being in transition; what I am going to teach you next is of critical importance if you wish to greatly improve your chances of Acing an Interview!

Getting To Know You

For most of you, getting to know who you *really* are and *what* you are capable of doing is going to be extremely hard.

The reason for this is that most people simply take *who* they are completely for granted. They go through life on "autopilot"; going about their day the same as the day before and the day before that - functioning robotically in a sea of mediocrity. Does this sound familiar?

Eventually the days become weeks, the weeks become months, then years and twenty years later, you are sitting in front of someone like me...looking nonplused when your Interviewer asks you what your greatest strengths are, what you ideally are looking for in your next position, or what you love to do most.

Difficult questions, right? Yes, they are if you have never given them much thought. You should never be thinking about how best to answer a question in an interview - that is way too late in the game.

The saddest fact, however, about taking *yourself* for granted is that in time, everyone around you will as well: your family, friends, colleagues, superiors, clients etc. - simply everyone because you will have taught them that you are nothing special, and *that* is the furthest thing from the truth!

Figure Out What You Love To Do

Why is it so important to figure out what you love to do? I know you must be thinking, "Why do I have to do this? It's such a pointless exercise!" I understand how you feel, but please bear with me...

We all have innate God-given talents, things that we love to do and so we lean in and do these things more often. Because of that, we become so good at doing these things that we do them automatically, and they give rise to our greatest strengths.

Knowing your greatest strengths is imperative to finding out what it is that you have to offer.

Several years ago, I was at a conference and during the event, the organizers had us do certain exercises to help us determine whether we were predominantly "left brained" (highly analytical types) or "right brained" (very creative types). The purpose of this exercise was to show everyone that no matter what you were, you could learn to be a little more like your opposite, and this would be very beneficial to learning new skills.

The presenter asked all "left brained" people to stand up and move to the left hand side of the classroom, and likewise then, asked the "right brained" people to stand up and move to the right side of the room.

There was a small group of us that were not exactly sure because we felt that we could go either way, so we remained seated. The presenter then told us that we were known as equally "left/right brained people." I was amazed that I had never heard of anyone being both left and right brained at the same time.

What puzzled me even more was that I was in this group and had never even known about it. I had often been told (not always in a complementary way!) that I was too analytical - but the people who often lamented that I was too analytical generally knew little else about me.

It was a really interesting conference with exposure to many new and interesting concepts, but nothing intrigued me more than finding out that I was equally left and right brained.

I came home and did some research on the Internet and found out that it was really not an uncommon phenomenon, but what plagued me most was that I had been completely unaware of this.

How could this be, that I never knew this about myself? So to find the answer, I kept going back further and further until eventually, I simply thought about what I loved doing most as a child and there it was! - The two subjects that I liked most at school, were Mathematics (which I found easy and fun, as I always saw trends, patterns, and logic in numbers) and Art (I simply loved drawing and painting).

Now to you this may seem frivolous and not terribly important to know - but I cannot tell you how much it made sense to me once I found out how *my* brain worked. Now I understood why I had made certain choices, and how completely natural and comfortable certain activities felt, while other tasks were downright difficult.

Nothing in life is a coincidence. Everything that happens to us has a reason and a purpose, but it is only with hindsight that we see and understand this.

When I was reading Walter Isaacson's biography of Steve Jobs, I remember him writing about how Steve dropped out of the course he was doing at Reed College. Steve then decided that he would return the following semester, but would only do the courses that he really liked. He casually dropped in one day on a Calligraphy class and loved it.

Many years later, when he was giving his famous Commencement Speech at Stanford University, he mentioned that because of that specific decision, Apple Computers had the most beautiful typography, and that's where he got the idea from.

Even seemingly small decisions made at a certain time in one's life can have enormous significance later on.

Finally, it is imperative that you work on this so that *you* know, with confidence and clarity, what it is that you bring to the table.

Interviewers are often extremely restricted in what they can legally ask a Candidate, and as privacy laws become more onerous, so do the associated restrictions imposed on us - so *you,* as the Candidate, need to offer this up.

Make a List of What You Don't Enjoy Doing

The above statement is self-explanatory - but don't let the simplicity of the task give you a free pass to *not* do it!

I cannot tell you how many times I have interviewed Candidates who, when asked what they really don't like doing or what their weaknesses are, looked at me like a deer caught in the headlights - as if it's the first time they have ever thought about it!

This makes you look like a fool, and you cannot afford that. Successful people always know what their strengths and weaknesses are, and more importantly, they have learned how to capitalize on their strengths and minimize their weaknesses. You can only do this if you know what yours are - so get busy on that list...

List Your Achievements and State Exactly What You Did to Accomplish Them

For this list, I really want you to go back in memory as far as you can, and think of every meaningful achievement, both personal and professional, that you realized. Then I want you to write down exactly what that involved, what you had to do, what sacrifices you made, and how you *felt* once you reached your goal!

You should also think of a problem or challenge that started off badly that you managed to turn around; note how you *felt,* and how incredibly relieved and proud you were to have been able to turn things around.

Write down what the problem was, what action steps you took, what you learned from the situation, and what the eventual outcome was. You may also want to mention the effect this turn of events had on your morale and that of your team.

Remember even the smallest detail may seem innocuous at the time, but may have undeniable eminence later on.

Commonly Asked Interview Questions

Clients basically want to know the following:

- Who are you and what do you have to offer them in the way of making their lives so much better?
- What do you know about their Company?
- Why are you interested in the position?
- Why do you want to leave your current position? Or why did you leave your last position if you are no longer employed?
- Can you solve their problems?
- Why should they hire you?

Whether these questions are direct questions, technical or behavioral in nature, they all have as their basic supposition, the inherent query - "What can you do for *them*?"

Remember, Interviewers represent the Company's interests and they always evaluate, and judge a Candidate from *their* perspective.

I will not insult your intelligence by listing 101 top interview questions, but I will say this, many of those questions are often similar questions paraphrased to look like a different question.

For example:

The question: Many people would love to work for our Company. Why should we hire you?

Could also be paraphrased as follows:

- Tell us why you think you are the best Candidate for the job?

- How would you distinguish yourself from the other shortlist Candidates?

- What attributes do you have that would convince us to hire you?

- This is a key role, and we are looking for someone really special - what would make us consider you?

- What strengths do you bring to the table and what past achievements can you draw on that would make it a no-brainer for us to hire you?

Do you see how many combinations and permutations there are to ask the same question; however, if you have done the work that I suggested, and you *really know who you are,* and *what you have to contribute*, you will never be stumped again!

For every opportunity that you consider submitting your Candidacy for - ask yourself this question, *every single time*:

"Why am I the best Candidate for the job?" Your answer should always start off with, "I can contribute immediately...because..."

and then list the myriad of reasons *why* you are able to contribute immediately - even if this is ONLY a thought process in your mind - it's exactly what you should be thinking!

You should approach every challenge, opportunity or problem, and look at it through this filter; the more often you do it - the more reasons you will find to justify your belief that you *really are* the best Candidate for the role.

This is how you build your confidence so that no matter what question is asked of you or how a question is asked, you will be able to answer from a position of strength, in a cool, calm, composed manner. This is how you hit your stride and take your Power back!

Action Steps

1. Work on those three lists. This will be the hardest and most labor intensive thing I ask you to do, but it is also the most critical. Without doing this, you will never know how amazing you are!

2. Craft your Cover Letter and Resume around the information you have gleaned about yourself. Do the same for your LinkedIn Profile and other Social Media Profiles.

3. Get really clear about what contributions you have to offer a Prospective Employer, and think continuously about what you can do for *them*, especially in terms of your problem solving skills. Remember, the best predictor of future success is past success.

CHAPTER 4

The Difference Between Contingency Recruiting And Retained Executive Search And Why This Makes A Difference To *You*, As A Candidate

"Hiring the best is your most important task."

Steve Jobs

I was recently talking to a CEO Candidate of mine who expressed the usual frustration that most people have when they are in transition, and are proactively looking for their next position.

"I never hear back from anyone," he said discouragingly. "Why don't people have the decency to get back to one?"

"I understand how you feel. Were you working with a Headhunter from a Retained Executive Search firm or with a Recruiter from an Agency?" I asked.

"What's the difference?" he enquired. I told him that there is a distinct difference, and proceeded to explain the differences, and how they affected him.

He listened attentively, and then said, "I feel like a fool! I never knew there was any difference."

Now, this person is a very accomplished Senior Executive, and if he doesn't know the difference, then I realized that it was definitely a topic that I needed to cover.

Referring to a Headhunter as a Recruiter is like calling a Chief Financial Officer a Bookkeeper. I realize that no offense is meant, but what many people don't know is that Executive Search is a recognized subspecialty of Management Consulting.

The most prestigious Executive Search firms hire their Search Consultants with graduate and postgraduate degrees, many with MBAs from Ivy League Universities. The education, skills, and years of experience that it takes to be at the top of one's game - is considerable, to say the least.

Recruiters generally work for Contingency Agencies, the meaning of which I will explain in detail shortly. Recruiters interview job applicants for lower level positions. They may even interview, and screen job seekers at the middle management level, and there are some Recruiters who even work at the Executive level.

Definition of Contingency Recruiting Agencies and How They Work

Contingency Firms (Recruiting Agencies) only get paid when, and if they present a Candidate that a Company subsequently hires; hence the name – Contingency. Based on this business model, Contingency Firms don't have the time and resources to actively source (headhunt), and pre-qualify only the most suitable Candidates for the position.

They will often do the following:

- Present whatever Candidates they have on their database that match most of the job description, and hope that the Candidates will satisfy the Client's criteria.

- Present as many Candidates as they can, since they do not have exclusive assignments and are in a race against other Agencies to present a winning Candidate.

- Market their most sought after Candidates, to multiple companies at the same time.

- Balance several assignments simultaneously, resulting in less attention given to both Candidates and Clients.

The Contingency recruiting process is quite simple. Recruiters learn the basic facts about the job vacancy (usually over the phone) or via email, scan their database for appropriately qualified Candidates, and submit their Resumes as quickly as possible.

Contingency Recruitment Firms will forward Resumes and perhaps a brief on a Candidate to the hiring Manager or the HR Manager at the Client Company.

Companies who work on this business model are always in a race against time <u>and</u> all the other Agencies who have the same "Job order" - so it becomes a "feeding frenzy" to get their Candidate's Resume to the Client as soon as possible.

Hopefully, the Client will hire *their* Candidate, and only then does the Agency get paid.

Pros and Cons

If a Candidate has lost their job, they may well believe that it would be to their advantage to be on as many Recruiting Firms' databases as possible. If you are a senior professional, this would be a grave mistake. Recruiting Agencies best suit lower level positions in the corporate environment.

A Professional person should always be concerned about their privacy, and their reputation.

Since a Recruiter from a Contingency Firm or Agency only gets paid once a Company hires their Candidate, they are only concerned with the *most* marketable Candidate, which inevitably does not serve a Candidate's interest.

A Recruiter who works on this basis always has to be concerned that *their* Candidate, does not know too much about the Company that they are being referred to for fear that they may speak to a Recruiter from a different Agency, and let valued information "slip" that the second Agency could use to get *their* own Candidate in for the same position.

Remember, Agencies who work on this business model don't have exclusivity with regards to the position.

This severely compromises the Candidate, in the following ways:

- Firstly, the Candidate does *not* know who the Company is that they are being referred to, until just before they go in for their interview. This could be a few days before (if you are extremely lucky) or the day before, depending on the Agency's policy.

- Therefore, the Candidate has no way of doing the required due diligence that is imperative to be successful; on the Company, key people, critical projects, recent news briefs on Fund Raisings, Mergers and Acquisitions, and other important events, etc.

- When you are in an interview, the Interviewer will more often than not *want* to know *what* you know about the Company. If you were only given minimal time to do your research, this will compromise your ability to be well informed, and it will show.

- As Agencies compete with each other constantly for the same positions, the Candidates who work with them are not competing against another two or three Candidates, short-listed for the same role, but with multiple unknown Candidates from several Agencies, so the pressure to beat out other Candidates has just gone up exponentially!

- Privacy: Your privacy can never be guaranteed - even though the Agency may swear blind that they do. Your private information will always be released to a Company before you know where your information has gone (unless you expressly state that they may not do so).

Finally your interviews will be rushed as the Recruiter just needs to establish whether you possess the Education, Skills, and Experience that match the checklist they received from the Company. If you're a match for most of those criteria, you're short-listed!

Rarely does the Recruiter have sufficient time to invest in a Candidate to build rapport and understand what is best for the Candidate in the long run - as opposed to what is best for the Recruiter, in the immediate term.

Definition of Retained Executive Search Firms and How They Work

Retained Executive Search Firms work on the same premise as Management Consultants. They enter into a contract with a Client Company, which clearly outlines the scope of the Search Assignment, cost and timeline. Retained Executive Search Firms are paid in retainers throughout the contract.

Retained Executive Search is the most appropriate method for procuring talent that is absolutely crucial, and strategic to the business of the Company, specifically when it is critical to hire not just any qualified person, but the most qualified, and best individual to meet the challenges of the position.

They will often do the following:

- Work exclusively on each Search Assignment - As a result, a Retained Executive Search Firm will never present the same Candidates to more than one Client at a time.

- Not "market" Candidates as they are being paid for the process of selecting the best Candidate for the Client, so they can be more objective about whether a particular individual is the right choice.

- Work exclusively for the Company, and focus on the specific needs of the business to ensure a qualified Candidate is identified for a position. They also offer only exclusive opportunities to their Candidates.

- Work with the Client to develop a highly detailed position specification and Corporate Profile. After this position specification has been developed, a comprehensive Search Strategy is planned.

- Often make a primary visit to the Client location to see the operations first-hand and meet as many people as they can, whose input will be relevant to the successful outcome of the Search Assignment.

- Provide the Client with comprehensive consulting and reporting, including Resumes on the short-list Candidates, references, interview notes, and full Candidate reports.

- Present three to five qualified Candidates.

- Guarantee confidentiality.

- Manage the closing negotiations and offer between the Client and the Candidate.

Pros and Cons

For most Senior Executives in transition, this is the better way to go (as opposed to working with a Recruiter). Later, I will offer what I believe to be the best method of finding the right position when you are looking for your next opportunity.

Advantages to Candidates would be as follows:

- You will be working with senior professional people who will take the time to understand you and find out what you want.

- If they feel that you are not suitable for a particular role, they will let you know and you will not be sent on interviews for which you are not suited as *they* have their reputation and credibility to lose.

- You will be able to build rapport with people who care and who are invested in your success because they understand that if you are successful, then they will be too.

- You are more likely to build a long-term relationship with a good Headhunter than with a Recruiter for the above mentioned reasons.

- You will have less competition per position than if you were referred by a Contingency Recruiter.

- Because you will know who the Company is, you'll certainly have more time to prepare - which will enable you to:

  1. Get into the right mindset of presenting yourself as "the best Candidate for the job"

  2. Develop a strategic approach on how you are "able to contribute immediately"

  3. Do thorough due diligence and find out everything there is to know about the Company and its major stakeholders

Disadvantages to Candidates would be as follows:

- The Executive Search Professional will still be on a very tight Client deadline and will have limited time for you. Few will do "Career Coaching" as time simply does not permit.

- Since the Company is paying them on retainer, they have a contract with the Client to deliver the best Candidate for the job on a timely basis - so their focus is on meeting the Client's expectations and that Client is *their* priority!

- As the Client is the Search Professionals priority, *you,* as the Candidate, might not even be a distant second. This is not meant to hurt you; it's simply the nature of the business. We have all been taught to "Pay the Piper" and focus on our highest earning opportunity.

- Even though each Search Assignment is exclusive and proprietary, many Executive Search Professionals have several simultaneous assignments on the go - so their time is at a premium.

- Executive Search Professionals are likely to travel extensively making them often inaccessible to an anxious Candidate who desperately needs a job!

As a Candidate, You should be able to ask any question relevant to the Job Search that you want to.

As mentioned previously, I work exclusively on a Retained Executive Search basis for the Corporations for whom I head-hunt senior professionals.

In addition to this, I provide Training to Job Seekers and do Private One-on-One Coaching with individuals who are my Private Coaching Clients.

During the late 1990's and just prior to and after the Millennium, I was working extensively in the niche market of Information Systems Security. A Corporate Client of mine had retained my services to headhunt several Senior IT Security Professionals.

During my research, a particular name emerged of a Candidate who was an Authority Expert in this field, and of course, I decided to approach him.

I called Bill and told him about my Client, the Company that I was working for, and filled him in regarding the details of the Company and the opportunity itself. I told him everything and gave him full access to all the information I had, thinking this would be sufficient for him to make a decision as to whether he was interested or not.

And then he did something that I never expected! He threw a curveball at me...

"Before I decide to work with you," he said, "I want to check you out! So, why don't you send me a list of *your* references and I will see whether *you* are good enough to work with me!"

Wow! - I thought; how's that for turning things around? No Candidate had ever had the audacity to say anything like that to me before.

I was stunned, but after a few seconds, I thought, well why not, "Sure," I said, while trying to expertly regain my composure, "I'll send you a list of reference contacts as soon as I have put down the phone, and you can check me out!"

"Fine," said Bill - unruffled, "I'll get back to you when I'm finished, and I'll let you know whether I want to work with you at all," and with that; he was finished with the conversation.

I sat in my chair dumbfounded...There's only one way to take this off the table, I thought; - give him what he wants.

Within half an hour, I fired off a list of my reference contacts and wondered whether he would even bother to call anyone or if it was simply a ruse to get rid of me...He was an IT Security Specialist after all, and probably more paranoid than most people who receive unsolicited calls from strangers.

My plate, however, was full, and I did not have much time to dwell further on what had just happened. So, not thinking that I would ever hear back from Bill, I continued working on my other assignments.

About eight days later, I received a call from a much more humbled and civilized Bill. "I've called your references and I would very much like to work with you"; he said.

We subsequently met; he turned out to be a very nice man and a great Candidate, and - yes, he did get the job!

The moral of the story is this...I realize that people who don't know one are naturally suspicious of strangers calling them with a proposition, even if it is a good one.

They need reassurance, and if the person calling is evasive and unwilling to answer questions or share information or gives clichéd responses like, "I can't tell you that because it's confidential," it's normal to think that they are hiding something!

People, who have nothing to hide, hide nothing - they don't lie and they aren't evasive!

So to give Bill the reassurance that he needed and deserved, I sent him my list of references. By doing so, it allowed him to feel that *he* was in control, and in the process he found out a lot more about me than I would ever, probably have told him directly.

He was able to corroborate independently *who* I was and *how* I worked, and in the course of doing this, developed a new level of respect for me.

This was further evidenced when, after a while at my Client, he later sought my services independently when he was again in a period of transition. Because I was honest right out of the gate, our relationship was based and built on truth and trust.

The Best Approach To A New Job Search - Doing It On Your Own

Earlier, I alluded to what I thought would be the *best* method of approaching a job search. This is it!

No matter whom you are working with - whether it is a Contingency Recruiter or a Retained Executive Search Professional, you absolutely cannot ignore this last, and what I believe to be the most important strategy for a job search - doing it on your own!

There are several reasons for this:

1. You become stronger and more independent when you take 100% responsibility for finding your own position.

2. If your technology and social media skills are a little outdated - it's a great time to hone them and learn new ones - necessity is the mother of invention!

3. It's an opportunity to enhance your networking skills, build new relationships, and forge new friendships.

4. You can do your own job search in tandem with other resources, such as working with Recruiters and Headhunters.

5. Never neglect doing this - because you give your power away when you place the onus of responsibility on someone else to find you a job!

6. You're able to keep the momentum going because *you* are in control of how many companies you choose to approach.

7. You become more knowledgeable about an industry or niche market, each time *you* do your own research.

8. Should you be hired directly through your own efforts; you will have learned more about the Company by doing your own due diligence than through second hand information, received from a third party.

9. If a Company hires you directly - you will have saved them a huge fee.

10. When you are fully responsible for your own job search - you approach things differently; you become more strategic, you learn more about everything, the industry, the companies, the key players, etc.

11. Most importantly - you learn about *yourself* and what *you* have to offer, and *why* you are the best Candidate for the job!

12. You don't leave things to chance. Your thinking shifts from worrying about how *many* other people you are competing with to *what* you have to offer.

13. You become stronger with every direct approach to a Company and you remove the inefficiencies and redundancies of wishing, waiting and hoping to hear back from others, who do not really have your best interests at heart.

Why this Makes a difference to you as a Candidate

1. You become stronger as you put more effort into building your self-confidence, honing your skills and building new ones, and in so doing, ultimately presenting yourself in a completely new way, a fuller, more complete package.

2. It's a much more strategic approach as you will be making direct contact with the companies of *your* choice.

3. It will be a case of quality versus quantity - in terms of your emotional and time investment.

4. You will have a greater ability to do proper, and more thorough due diligence, which,

5. Improves your knowledge of the Company, and this knowledge puts you in a much stronger position to define how you are going to present yourself.

6. Instead of worry about how many other Candidates you are competing against - you will focus your energy on why you *are* the best Candidate for the job!

© Randy Glasbergen
www.glasbergen.com

GLASBERGEN

"We're looking for someone with the wisdom of a 50 year old, the experience of a 40 year old, the drive of a 30 year old and the pay scale of a 20 year old."

Action Steps

1. Ask, Ask, Ask - Don't be afraid to ask any person who calls you with a job opportunity the following:

    *   Who *they* are and *what* Company *they* represent or work for?

    *   On what basis do they work? i.e. on a Contingency Basis or a Retained Executive Search Basis

    *   What are *their* credentials? Don't be afraid to check them out.

    *   What information about their Client are they prepared to share with you?

- You should be able to ask them anything about themselves and the Company that they are recruiting or headhunting for.

  If they are evasive or simply refuse to tell you or say that it's "confidential" - you should seriously consider whether you wish to give this person all *your* personal information or even deal with them. I'm just saying... My Candidates always get full disclosure.

2. Decide how you wish to approach your job search and who you wish to work with:

   - A Contingency Recruiter

   - A Retained Executive Search Professional

   - Through your own efforts - I am a huge proponent of Candidates taking their power back and doing their own research to find the Companies they wish to work for.

3. Once you have decided, based on the options you choose, develop a plan of action:

   - Remember to make what *you* have to offer a prospective Client, your highest priority in terms of having a list of well-substantiated successes.

   - Decide which companies you want to work for. Look at niche markets and at Fortune 500 listings of what companies have the best performance and highest ratings in terms of employee satisfaction. Also, look at websites such as www.glassdoor.com that offer information on Companies and Employee Reviews.

   - Keep doing relevant research into what *you* want in terms of your next position. Go deep into the companies that you want to work for, and the specific opportunity that would suit you best.

   - Network, network, network with pertinent people who are in a position to provide additional information, and often even referrals to key players. These are people that may well have influence in the companies that you are interested in.

- Your keen interest and enthusiasm can only serve you well and will not go unnoticed by those observing you. They may have more clout than you realize.

This should always be your strategy, irrespective of who you choose to work with, or whether you are doing it in tandem with a Headhunter looking out for you at the same time.

Remember, no-one will ever be more emotionally or financially invested in your success than you!

CHAPTER 5

The Executive
Search Process

"Great vision without great people is irrelevant."

Jim Collins

The following is an overview of the Executive Search Process, primarily used by Retained Executive Search Firms when head-hunting senior talent for their Clients. Most firms will have their own proprietary process and may have more or fewer steps in the process, but generally most firms will cover at least the following five stages outlined in this model.

I'm presenting this so that Candidates can see what is involved in terms of work, timing, and resources. Hopefully, it will help to explain why you are often left waiting, while the Executive Search Consultant is working furiously to keep to their own tight deadlines (often imposed by a Client's urgent needs).

An Executive Search Assignment can be an arduous process and when you, as the Candidate, know what is involved; hopefully, you'll understand that it could be a few weeks before your next contact with your Search Consultant. Even so, I believe

Candidates should always be apprised as to the timing of the process.

**"I've hit the glass ceiling so many times,
my hair smells like Windex."**

The Five Stages Of The Executive Search Process

Planning

The Planning Stage is generally the most crucial in the Executive Search Process. It is in this stage that the Search Firm learns more about the Client's organization, corporate culture, business objectives, mission, and goals for the future.

The Search Consultant will engage in discussion with the Client about the business issues that, they are facing in their marketplace, and help them identify the vital characteristics that the desired individual should have in order to meet those specific challenges.

The Search Consultant will take a pro-active approach in helping the Client identify and qualify the core competencies and characteristics that the successful Candidate should possess in order to be successful in the role.

It is also during this phase that the Search Consultant will discuss their Firm's Search Strategy, scope of the assignment, timeline, and fee for the assignment, and answer all questions that a Client may have.

Candidate Identification

During this phase, suitable Candidates (often used as "point of reference" Candidates) are contacted in a discreet and confidential manner to assess their interest and suitability for the opportunity.

A Search Firm may also elect to advertise the position, if that's what the Client wants. Each Search Assignment is proprietary to every Company and how the search is run will depend on what is best for that particular Company. Every part of the process is a collaboration between the Client and Search Firm.

Once a "collective group" of the most qualified Candidates have been identified – based on their qualifications, skills, experience, and suitability for the position; they are contacted to assess *their* level of interest.

Candidate Evaluation

Candidates selected for further consideration are considered to be "long-list" Candidates, and they are given in-depth interviews to further assess their suitability for the role and compatibility with the Client's corporate culture.

The Search Firm will also try and ascertain whether the individual's goals and objectives are in alignment with the Client's business objectives.

This long-list of Candidates is further culled to the top 3-5 individuals, who are then discussed with the Client and moved to a short-list, as they represent the very best Candidates, for the position.

Then, extensive reference checking is done to verify work history, strengths, desirable characteristics, suitability, and to confirm past achievements and their ability to handle similar challenges and business issues relevant to the Client's organization.

The Client is then presented with a detailed final report covering the entire search process, specific findings, and comprehensive details on the short-listed Candidates

Final Selection

During this stage, the Executive Search Consultant will serve as the "liaison" between the Client and the Candidates and set up meetings, culminating with the finalist interviews.

The Executive Search Consultant will often guide and counsel a Client or the Search Committee on the appropriate protocol for interviews with the Candidates; advising on a strategy for evaluating Candidates in terms of the selection criteria chosen at the outset of the Search Assignment.

The Executive Search Consultant will also assist in the negotiation of the offer of employment, so that the transition for the successful Candidate to their new environment is a seamless and pleasant experience.

Integration and Follow Up

The real measure of success is a satisfied Client and a happy and enthusiastic Candidate.

The Search Assignment doesn't end when the Candidate starts working; it ends when the new incumbent's tenure and performance successfully passes the test of time.

Most Executive Search Consultants will follow up with both the Candidate and Client at regular intervals to assess performance and manage any possible issues that may arise.

Action Steps

1. If you have not already done so, Craft your Resume, Cover Letter, and one Page Synopsis of your Resume.

   Also have a list of your major strengths and accomplishments, substantiated by clear-cut examples. This helps you to know what specific positions suit you best.

   Know what industry you want to work in and what kind of Company you want to work for - their Core Values should align with yours. Most reputable companies do have a set of Core Values that are often posted on the Company's website.

   Look at websites such as: http://www.glassdoor.com to see whether the Company that you want to work for is listed. Research what current and former employees are saying about the organization.

2. Social Media - Make time to update your LinkedIn page and "clean-up" your Facebook page; the same goes for your "tweets". Make sure that your Social Media presence presents you in the best possible light.

3. Enlist the help of a third party to review what you have done. This person should preferably be a professional person who can give you unbiased feedback and constructive criticism to help you improve the way you present yourself to the outside world, both on paper and Social Media.

CHAPTER 6

Why You Need To Be Prepared For Every Phase Of The Executive Search Process

"The Future belongs to the competent.
It belongs to those who are very, very good at what they do.
It does not belong to the well-meaning."

Brian Tracy

A few years ago, I was going through an incredibly busy period. Generally I am always busy, but this season seemed to be much more hectic than usual and it was during this time that a particular Candidate kept calling me.

It was also after I had just moved down to Washington State. He wanted to see me in Vancouver, British Columbia, a city I did visit on a fairly regular basis, but at the time, I had no plans to specially cross the border to meet with him.

He was not a shortlist Candidate, but someone who had simply sent me his Resume on an unsolicited basis. Normally, I do not see anyone on an unsolicited basis, but he was so persistent, and since I had put him off for a while, the guilt was starting to seep in.

Would it be so terrible if I simply made some time for him the next time I was in Vancouver? I thought. Trying to kill two birds with one stone, I agreed to see him at a restaurant in between my other Client calls; the next time I was in the city.

I did have his Resume and had given it a quick cursory glance (this was entirely my fault - you see even Headhunters need to be prepared and I was not).

We had lunch and then I interviewed him with the usual scrutiny and in-depth attention that I give to other Candidates.

I became increasingly appalled the more I interviewed and the deeper I dug. The time periods on his Resume did not run consecutively and there were times where he had no work record at all.

When I asked him to fill in what he had done during these times, he became flippant, thinking he could charm his way out of this. I was annoyed and let him know that he was wasting my time (but secretly, I was really angry with myself - a little preparation of a few minutes could have saved me the time and trouble of seeing him at all).

The fake charm morphed into evasion and then eventually stone walling as he became passive aggressive. I told him that if he was not prepared to be honest, I could not represent him and ended the interview.

However, it was also a learning experience for me; to slow down - to achieve more.

Often, we are so rushed that we make mistakes and things need to be redone. Redoing anything takes longer than doing it right the first time.

Most Candidates generally are unprepared when they see a Headhunter. The feeling I get is that Candidates believe the onus is on the Headhunter to do the work. There is almost an unspoken expectation that the Interviewer will let the Candidate know whether their Resume and Cover Letter are good enough and in certain instances, when it isn't - once again the expectation is that the Headhunter has to "fix it up."

I once had a Candidate scream at me in the most belligerent way when I asked him to redo his Resume. He refused, saying that if I wanted it changed, *I* should do it since it was good enough for him and every other person who had interviewed him before!

Let's be clear - it's *your* career we are talking about, and the onus is on *you* to represent yourself to best advantage. Just because your Accountant prepares your Tax Return does not mean he is also responsible for paying your taxes.

Now, there is nothing wrong with asking for an honest critique, and I'm sure that would never be met with "I can't" or "That's not my responsibility."

Any Recruiter, HR Person, or Headhunter of repute would gladly give you some free and friendly advice if asked. If your paperwork is really bad, but you are an excellent Candidate, they will usually volunteer some helpful, unsolicited advice on their own to assist you in presenting yourself more favorably.

Then there are some "dream" Candidates who are in strong contrast to the Candidate I mentioned at the beginning of this chapter.

Several years ago, I was retained by an international Company with offices in Canada, Australia and Vietnam to find certain highly skilled talent in a hot and booming resource market.

So even though I was interviewing Candidates in Canada, the expectation was that the actual positions were in Vietnam. The Candidates knew this and were eager for the opportunity as it was a really good Company with excellent prospects, and for many, the chance to get very valuable international experience.

One such Candidate was Leon. He submitted his Candidacy for one of the senior positions. There were, however, many Candidates interested for the reasons previously mentioned, but he was special.

His Resume was excellent and the accompanying Cover letter was impeccably done in terms of mentioning exactly the appropriate content, right experience, why he was interested, and what he could do for my Client.

We subsequently teed up a meeting and had an interview, which only further reassured me that he was definitely the best Candidate for the position. I did, however, have some very good back-up Candidates as well.

Later, I flew to Vietnam when I was ready to present all Candidates for the various positions to my client contact - the Chief Operating Officer (COO). We discussed the Candidates at length for the different positions and it was left that he would get back to me with the Candidates that the Company wanted to pursue.

The COO was also a "dream" Client. True to his word, he got back to me swiftly with the names of Candidates that the Company was interested in. Leon was on the list.

As I had placed another senior specialist with the Company the year before, it was arranged that when he was back in Toronto, he would meet with Leon. The two met and the meeting seemed to go well. Two weeks later, Leon was flown out to Vietnam.

I was not expecting to hear anything until after he got back, so I was quite surprised when a mere three days later, I got a one line email from the COO that simply stated, "I have decided to make Leon an offer." I could not wait to hear back from Leon to find out exactly what happened.

He returned to Canada from his interview and called to give me feedback. Leon told me that he was shown around the operations and realized that there were inefficiencies that were costing the Company money.

Leon identified different areas where he felt changes could be implemented that would result in a better yield and recovery of the ore, which in turn decreased the cost and increased profitability of the operation. Leon felt that he could really contribute in a meaningful way.

He told the senior management team that were interviewing him, what he was doing in his current position (Leon was working for one of the biggest names in the industry) and how they had tackled similar problems to what my Client was seeing in their operation. He spoke to the Senior Executives that he met, about how his existing Company had addressed comparable issues, and how they had turned the situation around.

Before he left to come back home, he reiterated that he would love to work for the Company, and that he believed he could make a difference! In essence, he closed the deal. It was a "no brainer" for the Client to make him an offer.

Do you see that Leon was completely prepared? He was prepared from the "get go" - not just for the interview with my Client, but he was prepared for when he would receive the first call from me. I never, ever caught him off guard; he was always happy to hear from me, almost as if he was expecting my call, and he was ready for any question that I asked, and I ask plenty of questions!

I learned something so valuable from Tony Robbins that I often quote him because I believe it is true, "How you do *anything* is how you do *everything*!"

Leon's execution with whatever he did was flawless - from his Cover Letter and Resume to a great interview with me, followed on by successful meetings with other Executives, to the final interview with the Client in Vietnam. He also had superb references, which further corroborated how accomplished he was at his job.

Leon worked for my Client for a few years and eventually left when there was a change in Management. Later, when there was a downturn in this sector, he was never without work. People that he had worked for formerly, always got in touch with him, to offer him work, as soon as word got around that he was on the market.

When you're hot, you're hot! With effort, everyone can get there. The first caveat is that you have to *want* to better yourself, and the second caveat is that you have to be *prepared.*

Preparation For The Various Types of Interviews and Building Your Brand And Profile Through The Use Of Social Media

You could be approached by various kinds of people through different sources of media, and you need to be prepared for all of them.

There are many different "Tools" for Social Media, but for the purposes of showing you how to improve your chances of being found, and then seen in the most favorable light, I will cover the three main Tools that most of us are familiar with: LinkedIn, Facebook and Twitter.

The entire dynamic of interviewing and Job Search has completely changed with the advent of Social Media. Initially, Social Media (I mean specifically Facebook) was only used for personal reasons, but as the different Social Media companies evolved (think, LinkedIn and Twitter), so did their uses for business. Today, you can search someone on Google, and their Facebook, LinkedIn Page, Twitter Account, and other associated websites will pop up.

What was once confidential and sacrosanct information is now in the Public Domain for everyone to see. Employers are using these Tools to investigate and research an individual long before they ever meet him or her.

If you do not match up to a prospective Employer's criteria for a particular job search, forget about them ever reaching out to you. Now the good news is the corollary to this is also true; should you have a great profile, you may be contacted out of the blue with a surprisingly wonderful business proposition or offer.

After we have covered what you need to do on LinkedIn, Facebook and Twitter to improve your chances of being found and possibly getting a job offer, we will move on to the more traditional forms of interviewing: Telephone and Skype Calls (for initial screening) and then Face-to-Face interviews (which I will cover in the next Chapter) for more in-depth discovery.

For the sake of clarity and brevity, I have given you the basics of what you need to know and do to improve your Social Media image.

This book is called *Ace Your C-Suite Interview,* and I want to stick to the spirit of the message, which is all encompassing in regard to getting the job you want.

That being said, I also want to introduce you to the best information I have on the topic, so I turned to Authority Experts in this area, Joshua Waldman, Founder and CEO of Career Enlightenment: http://careerenlightenment.com and Shanna Landolt, CEO of the Landolt Group: http://landoltgroup.com

The information below is a combination of advice put out by LinkedIn, articles on the Internet (about how to get a job using Twitter and Facebook), and also information gleaned from the two authors mentioned above.

If you wish to become an "expert" on Social Media, by all means delve deeper. I strongly encourage all learning, and it's always great to hone your skills. It will only serve you better to know as much as possible in an ever changing dynamic like this.

1. LinkedIn

Make sure that your Profile is complete - Take time with this to really put effort into doing this as well as you can.

Your Profile should never be a rehash of what is on your Resume; rather, craft your Profile with the desired end result in mind - a Job interview!

Your Profile should be a short summary (5 - 10 lines) of who you are, what you love to do, and how well you are able to do it.

According to Joshua Waldman, your Profile (from the Interviewer's perspective) should always answer these 3 questions:

1. Do I like you?

2. Are you motivated?

3. Can you do the job?

So, when writing your Profile, remember to highlight the fact that you have an amiable personality; make sure that you come across as likeable, even humorous, but in a clean, nice way.

People love to work with others who are fun! Most people spend more time at work than at home - so everyone wants to be around someone who is happy, positive, and upbeat!

You also have to show that you are highly motivated and energetic! Remember that list of "strengths" that you were supposed to do? *That* list would really come in handy now...

Finally, to answer the third question, remember that *other* list of "well-substantiated success"... Yes! *That* list will help you to answer the third question.

Add a Profile Photo - adding a photo makes your profile 9 times more likely to be picked up in searches.

Your Profile picture should be relevant and professional!

I cannot tell you how many pictures I have seen on LinkedIn, a Social site for professionals, where guys (yes, especially men do this) post pictures of their Porsche or Ferrari.

This is also not the place to break out the family photos or cute pictures of your kids, dog, cat, or exotic lizard.

If you are seriously looking for a position, then your Profile picture should be approximately the size of your Passport picture with you, well dressed and smiling.

List all the Jobs and Positions that you've held, along with the descriptions of your roles. Did you know that having your two most recent positions listed makes your Profile twelve times more likely to be found?

Fill out your Industry details, where you worked, etc.

List your Education, Professional Designations, and where you studied.

Have at least 50 connections, but more is better, so add on members that you know, and reach out to those who share your business interests.

Recommendations and Endorsements: Life works on a *quid pro quo* basis. How many recommendations have you received and how many have you given? The person viewing your profile will be looking at this.

Groups: It is important to be active in Groups that are relevant to your Industry and business interests.

2. Facebook

Facebook is great for referrals of job leads, and currently more people are getting jobs through referrals on Facebook than through LinkedIn.

Recruiters and Business people are using Facebook to find prospective Candidates and vet them.

If you want to use Facebook for this purpose (and I don't know why you wouldn't if you were looking for a job), then you'll also have to take time to carefully do a really good and well thought out Profile - much as you did before.

Fill out your Profile with your Professional History, Work, and Education

Expand your network through using the Advanced Search Tool to reach out to people that you know at some of your "Target" companies. You should also be using this tool to find out more about the Companies that you wish to work for.

"Like" those Companies; share some of the most relevant posts that you think others in your network may enjoy, and comment on really good posts.

Post Content and Respond to Other People's Content.
Post Updates about Personal and Company accomplishments.

Pay Attention to Professional Friends' postings and "Like" their updates; make appropriate and complimentary comments wherever you can. Remember the power of Reciprocity!

3. Twitter

Twitter is a great resource for people finding you who may never have known that you even existed and can be a wonderful addition to your Job Search Strategy. Here are a few ways to stay relevant and current:

Share things that you find professionally interesting, along with a link to the article and a couple of relevant hashtags.

Find the latest Job openings - Make a point of following Recruiters who specialize in your Industry and Companies that you would like to work for.

Stay up to date with your Industry and Profession - Most Professional Associations will tweet about upcoming meetings and conferences and these can often be great networking opportunities.

Follow Key Leaders in Business that interest you - these people use Twitter to promote their companies, which affords you incredible inside information that may be helpful to your Job Search.

4. Telephone Interview

Make sure that you are up, showered, and well dressed for your Telephone Interview. I can just hear you say, "Really? That's ridiculous - no one can see me!"

Remember, change happens from the inside out…and for many people in transition, getting out of bed in the morning, showered and properly dressed, is an accomplishment. It may well seem like a minor one, but an accomplishment none the less, and you should build on every achievement to make yourself feel better.

Please don't knock this until you've tried it! Honestly, you will feel so much more wide awake and keen to do something motivating or fun after the interview (particularly if it went well) as you are already dressed and ready to greet the day!

Under no circumstances should you ever interview in your pajamas, even though you have convinced yourself that it is physically impossible for anyone to see you and know this. The Interviewer will be able to "feel" and "sense" your lethargy and laid back demeanor.

Most Interviewers are very experienced at what they do and you will never know what they think about you, but you will be quickly written off if you don't come across as "bright eyed and bushy tailed".

Now, if you have just rolled out of bed and fallen on your face (after a heavy night of drinking) minutes before your interview, this could be a particularly difficult miracle to pull off!

You also need to be well prepared for the interview - this goes without saying, but it would be remiss of me if I did not repeat myself here.

Make sure that you know the following so well that no Interviewer will be able to stump you on any question.

Know what you are looking for in terms of the following:

- The industry in which you want to work.

- The Company that you are interested in. Be able to explain why you are interested in *that* Company.

- Why you want to leave your current Company or why you are currently unemployed.

- Specifics of the Role that you would like and would suit you best.

- An in-depth knowledge of the Company, its leadership, competitors and major stakeholders, latest news releases etc. Don't be tardy about doing your homework.

- Any personal or professional contacts already working for the Company.

- Have a list of your strengths, major achievements (such as awards won and situations that you turned around, problems that you solved) and even a (small) list of weaknesses should you be asked.

Remember, never denigrate yourself, always turn a negative into a positive, and always end your response on an "inspiringly positive" note!

Example:

Interviewer: Can you give me an example of one of your biggest weaknesses?

Your response: I was not particularly savvy when it came to Social Media and hardly ever updated my LinkedIn profile. I worked so hard and there wasn't much time for that sort of thing.

However, since I was downsized, I went on the Internet and realized that Job Search has changed drastically from when I was last on the market.

So, I made it my priority to learn as much as I could and become an expert in Social Media. I've enrolled in several courses, and in a very short period of time, I have already learned a tremendous amount. It feels great to know I am much more astute in this area than I realized, and I'm really enjoying this!

It's OK to have these lists in front of you, so that you can refer to them if need be, but know *where* to find the information in an instant if you *have* to look at your notes.

You don't want to keep the Interviewer waiting for your answer while you scan through your notes - that would be another good reason to be wide awake when you take the call.

I cannot stress enough how important good preparation is to every facet of an interview.

You can easily be found on Social Media by improving your Professional Profile, and hence your chances of being found - BUT you will still have to have an interview.

It is how you conduct yourself during an interview that determines whether you move forward to the next round or get nixed.

"She brushed out my tangles, shampooed my fur and trimmed my nails. I think they're grooming me for a management position."

5. Skype Call

Everything that applies to the Telephone Call also applies to the Skype Call with a few additional caveats.

For this type of Interview, you can be seen, so I want you to dress in a business suit, white shirt and a well-coordinated tie.

For my female professionals and executives, the appropriate attire would also be a business suit or smart jacket, blouse, and skirt or long pants - whatever you prefer.

The general idea is to give the impression that you know what is appropriate and how to dress accordingly. Also, when you are dressed in business attire, you send a message that you are taking the process seriously and giving the Interviewer the respect that they deserve.

When I suggest a business suit, I mean the whole suit (including the pants). I know that it may be much more comfortable to put on just a shirt, tie, and jacket with nothing on underneath except boxers.

It is a Skype interview after all, right? - so who would know if you aren't wearing pants, when only your top half is visible and you are comfortably seated at a desk or table when you get the call?

Well, strange things happen during interviews. In the next chapter, I will regale you with yet more stories - so do stay tuned, but for now, let's get back to the Skype interview.

Imagine if you will the following scenario…

You are seated in front of your computer or laptop, fully engaged in your interview, when your darling wife walks into the room to give you a nice hot mug of coffee.

You are delighted to see her, and during the quick exchange some hot coffee falls on a rather compromising spot - you instinctively jump up to mitigate the damage and stifle a painful cry and a few choice words.

However right now, I am more worried about what the hapless Interviewer can see rather than what comes out of your mouth. It's at times like these that I pray you are at *least* wearing those boxers…

Your mortified Interviewer has now, by default, gotten to know you so much better and more intimately than ever intended.

Please, take my words to heart when I say wear a suit - I do mean the whole suit!

As you can be seen, there are a few things to bear in mind. You should preferably have the camera lens a little higher than your head; you don't want to be looking down into the camera.

This is a very unflattering angle for anyone, and you don't want someone looking up your nose – very uncomplimentary. I know these details seem petty, but people get grossed out easily, and I don't want that to be because of something you've done.

Remember, how you do anything is how you do everything!

When you are having a Skype interview, make sure that the space around you is very neat. You don't want to give the impression that you live in a pigsty and are highly disorganized. These seemingly small details could cost you the job, so don't give anyone cause to think that.

It is fine to have your Resume, Cover Letter, and other supporting documents with you, in case you need to refer to them. However, it would be even better if you were so familiar with your own background and career that you do not have to refer to them at all.

You also want to be enthusiastic, friendly, and warm. Thank the Interviewer at both the beginning of the interview for their time and again afterwards. Make sure that you pronounce their name properly, and if you are in any doubt as to the correct spelling of their name - ask them. You will appear interested in them, and your attention to detail will be noticed. You also need this information for your follow-up "Thank You" email after the interview.

Do ask the Interviewer whether it would be alright with them if you took some brief notes during the interview, but don't take such copious notes that your head is down all the time, and you forget to look up and make eye contact. Looking up and making eye contact is imperative for your Interviewer to be able to assess you. They want to see how you behave and communicate.

Remember, they are evaluating you *all* the time.

Ask relevant questions about the Company, position, key stakeholders, competitors, and any specific issues that your Interviewer may have mentioned or that your pre-interview research has uncovered.

Finally, remember to thank the Interviewer again when the interview is over. You may ask about next steps and reiterate your interest in the Company and position, BUT never ask about Salary - this is neither the time nor place, and far too early in the search process.

Your objective is simply to impress your Interviewer to such an extent that they are keen to have you meet more Hiring Managers and Senior Executives in the Company.

The final take away is, keep it classy and professional. You still want to be in the race and move to the next stage of the process, which will be a face-to-face interview.

What To Do Immediately After Your Phone or Skype Interview

- Do a post mortem of the interview - note what was asked, think about how you answered - were you pleased with the answers that you gave? Think about everything; make notes about what you felt was relevant for follow up, and what you could have done better on.

- Discuss the interview with a close friend or trusted professional advisor who will give you an independent, unbiased, objective opinion.

- Within 24 Hours, or as soon as you can afterwards (do not wait to do this), draft a "Thank You" email. Note, I said "draft" - I do want you to write what you wanted in your own voice. Thank the Interviewer for their time. Mention specifics that were discussed, assuring your Interviewer that you are still very interested, in both the Company and position, and see yourself as a good fit who could definitely help them with any challenges they may be having.

- Then discuss that draft "Thank You" note with your trusted advisor and get their opinion. Make any suggested edits, and when you are satisfied with the final result –

Then send off your email, but do this within a day of your interview.

You may not know this, but your Interviewer is "expecting" that follow up "Thank You" note. This is also another opportunity for you to make yourself more memorable and reaffirm your interest, and commitment to the Company and position.

Action Steps

1. Now that I have given you an overview of the different kinds of interviews, and you know which one you are having, prepare accordingly for it. Don't ever forget the initial preparation, such as knowing what kind of job you want, the Company details, and information on key people; prepare as expansively as you can for this.

2. Know what you have to offer - And also "Why you are the best Candidate for the job."

3. Always put yourself in the Interviewer's shoes, and think logically, about what would be most important to them. Then draw on what you have done - i.e. Your past achievements and problem solving skills. Remember your follow up "Thank You" email afterwards.

   Always appear interested, energetic, and motivated!

   Hiring the right people is an enormous investment for a Company, both in terms of time and money, so no-one wants to make a mistake!

CHAPTER 7

Detailed Preparation For The Final Interview

"By failing to prepare, you are preparing to fail."

Benjamin Franklin

The "Final Interview" may often not be the final interview, but it is often referred to as such by Executive Search Professionals or Headhunters to distinguish the specific day that the Panel or Executive Search Committee get together to interview and evaluate the short-listed Candidates for a particular Position.

Usually, the top selected Candidate, or even the top two selected Candidates (from those previously short-listed, seen, and interviewed), will be brought back to the Company to be shown around, and very possibly to meet and be interviewed by additional key people that perhaps were not part of the original Panel or Executive Search Committee.

In any event, there is a tremendous amount of preparation to do at different stages of the process:

Pre-interview Stage: (most of the prep takes place here)

- These are all the things we covered in the previous chapters, i.e. the lists that I tasked you with doing.

- If you are working with a Recruiter, Headhunter, or doing this on your own and now know that you have an interview coming up with a specific Company on *your* "Target" list - then this is the time to do extensive due diligence on the Company and the individuals that you will be meeting.

- This would also be a good time to check out the Company's competitors and relevant news stories; this will demonstrate that you have really taken the time to show how interested and invested you are.

A week before the interview:

- Whatever you have not covered from the above list - do so now!

- Make a point of getting the contact information of everyone that *you* are dealing directly or interviewing with, and make sure *they* have all *your* contact information. Do not assume anything.

  Unforeseen emergencies can crop up, and they are always at the last moment and most inconvenient time. Be prepared. Don't think that because the information is on *your* Resume, someone will have it with them.

  Communication flows both ways; however you, as the Candidate, must make sure that the Company has your information and you have the Company's information. The onus is on you!

- If you are having your interview in a city other than where you live, confirm your hotel booking and ask for a confirmation email so that when you get to the hotel, you can prove that you have a confirmed booking. You'll thank me for this later...

- Check your airline tickets and any pre-arranged transport etc.

- Confirm with the Company that you know exactly where the interviews are being held. Sometimes, a Company will choose to interview at a hotel and not at their offices. Ensure that you have the correct address.

- Make sure that you are not out of business cards. It looks very unprofessional when a business person has run out of cards or forgotten them at home.

- Go through your wardrobe, and ensure that the outfit you intend wearing is clean. If it needs dry-cleaning, now is the time to get this done - the day before is too late.

The Day before the interview:

- Think - don't drink.
- No Night Clubbing or Recreational Drugs.
- Last minute preparation in terms of your final due diligence, notes etc.
- If you are flying out to interview in another city:

   Make sure you have a check-list of everything you need: your clothes, shoes, toiletries, business cards, cell phone, charger, laptop, and iPad, etc.

   Take additional hard copies of your Cover Letter and Resume for the Panel or the Interviewer. They should have this information, but people lose and mislay things; *you* be prepared!

   Take your Air Ticket, Hotel Confirmation, Passport, and information on your Transport arrangements with you – don't put it in your checked luggage.

   Have a notebook with a list of questions that you may want to ask the Interviewer or Panel

Most of my Executive Search Assignments are either national or international in nature, so I am often dealing with unforeseen emergencies like Candidate's travel arrangements going awry due to inclement weather, people missing planes, or Clients changing the interview schedule.

I once had an international Client change arrangements at the last minute, while the Candidates were still in transit flying to the interview and then reschedule the interviews at ridiculous hours.

This resulted in one of my Candidates interviewing at 2:30 a.m.! I was not impressed, but the Candidate was a real trooper, took it in his stride, and never skipped a beat. He behaved like a true professional.

I have learned that you simply cannot prepare for every eventuality, but being well prepared, for most situations and obvious outcomes, certainly relieves a lot of stress.

This segues into another story and a very important point that I want to discuss. A few years ago, I was staying at the Bellagio Hotel in Las Vegas when the phone suddenly rang in the early hours of the morning.

I picked up the phone immediately. A small, soft, almost child-like voice implored me to, "Please come and get me! I'm waiting for you at the bottom of the elevators, and the security guards won't let me come up - so you have to come down and fetch me."

I was shocked, but fortunately fully awake by now and realized immediately that she had misdialed or gotten the room number wrong. "You have the wrong number," I replied and put down the phone quietly.

However, I was not alone on this trip for a little rest and recreation, no siree; my darling mother, who had come with for a treat to Las Vegas and who had been snoring quietly in the next bed, was now sitting bolt upright. The sharp ring of the phone had abruptly woken her up.

"Is everything alright?" she inquired, concerned. "Did anybody die?"

"No, Mom," I replied, "everything's fine."

"Who was that?" she asked.

"A prostitute," I replied calmly.

"What did she want?" - asked my mother with deeper concern.

"She wanted me to go down and fetch her... You know how the Security Guards check our key cards to make sure we are legitimate guests in the hotel; well she needs me to fetch her because she's not exactly a guest in the hotel!" - I could feel the mirth rising in my stomach and for my own gratuitous pleasure wanted to keep the joke going.

"What?" - shouted my mother incredulously, "Why did *you* call a prostitute!!?"

"I *didn't* call a prostitute! It was time to wrap up the joke. "Some guy must have called an Agency, and she was sent over, but probably got the room number wrong."

"Oh," said my mother, relieved and satisfied, as she rolled over and went back to sleep.

However, I was now wide awake and could not stop thinking; do my Candidates do this when they are away from home?

With many of my Search Assignments, there are often Candidates that have to fly in from out of town. Being in a city where one is completely unknown provides a certain degree of safety and anonymity. One can engage in certain forbidden delights which would be much more difficult to get away with at home.

My admonition: Even if you believe you can get away with this - don't do it!

As the Executive Search Consultant, I'm the Facilitator on the Panel of the Finalist interviews, and have often wondered why certain Candidates look so exhausted and spent when I know that they flew into town the day before and had plenty of time to decompress and rest.

If you've worked so hard to make a great impression for a job that you truly want, why blow your chances now? It's foolish!

The day of the Final (shortlist) Interview (or first face-to-face interview)

Your first face-to-face interview could be with a Headhunter, HR Manager, Senior Line Manager or an Executive of the Company. It could even be with a Panel (also known as the Search Committee).

- Get ready for your interview with plenty of time to spare. How you prepare mentally is also very important.

- Meditate; if that's not your thing or you don't know how to do it - simply sit quietly with your eyes closed in a chair and imagine how you would love the interview to go.

- Remember, things don't always go badly, sometimes they go amazingly well - but the mental rehearsal of how you'd like it to turn out is a very big part of the outcome.

- If you are still feeling a little nervous, that's perfectly normal and often a good thing; it means your creative juices are flowing and you're psyched for what lies ahead.

- If you are feeling incredibly tense, go for a walk; it will calm you down.

- Dress Code: Cleanliness really is next to Godliness. Be clean, neat in appearance, and look as if you have taken great care with your appearance. It counts.

If you are still not quite sure if your dress code is appropriate, a great way to make sure that you really do have the professional look down pat is to observe how the Anchors and Hosts on TV present themselves.

The interview process, for most companies, is generally formal: a dark business suit, crisp white shirt (which looks good on everyone) and a tie that tones in well - either a solid color or striped.

For women, the dress code is also business attire, pants suit, or dress and skirt, whichever you are most comfortable with.

Jewelry should be understated. If in doubt, always err on the side of being conservative.

Once you are gainfully employed by the Company, feel free to be more liberal and adventurous in your style!

- Cover Letter, Resume & Supporting Documents: Take additional copies with you to the interview.

  Often, the Headhunter on a Retained Search will have ensured that each member of the Panel has a complete Report on the whole Search Assignment, which will include detailed information on each short-listed Candidate.

  However, if you have found this opportunity on your own, you cannot assume that people are organized (trust me - don't assume anything!); be thoroughly prepared for yourself and everyone else

- Business Cards: You should always carry yours with you and remember to ask for your Interviewer's business card.

  If you are having a Panel interview, when you take a moment to thank them afterwards, also ask each person on the Panel if you may have a business card. You will need this information for your "Thank You" notes.

- Know the name of the person who will be interviewing you, or names of people, if it is a Panel interview; it's very important to address people by their correct name.

  It will also show that you pay attention to detail. Remember, everyone loves to be acknowledged, and remembering someone's name (and pronouncing it properly) will certainly make a good impression.

Find out as much as you can about the Interviewer, or the people on the Panel Interview (i.e. the Search Committee): their titles, background, tenure with the Company, special achievements, awards etc. everything that you can – and where appropriate offer a compliment, to the person who will be interviewing you.

A compliment always warms an Interviewer to the Candidate; look for reasons to make that connection, but always be honest, sincere and professional.

- Location: Make sure you know exactly where the interview is and, if necessary, drive there a day or so ahead of your interview, so that you have plenty of time to get there, factor in traffic, and budget your time for unforeseen emergencies.

- Arrive early, at least 15 minutes before your scheduled appointment. If you have more time to kill, take a walk around the block - the fresh air will do you good and the walk will be relaxing.

- Be warm and friendly to everyone you see (especially the Receptionist and the Executive Assistants you see floating around) - you will be amazed how many times their opinion is sought and valued by their bosses.

- When you are called in for your interview: Smile, look happy, and make great eye-contact with your Interviewer or the members of the Panel.

- Have a firm handshake, not a death-grip or a "wet fish" type of hand shake. It is best to mirror the handshake of the other person.

However, if the other person's handshake is weak, yours should be firmer, but don't crack their knuckles and break their fingers - nothing is more unfriendly than sending someone to the emergency room.

I have a firm handshake for a woman; however, early on in my career, when I first started in the industry, I worked for a big Search Firm.

One of my Colleagues at the time had a Candidate whom he wanted me to meet, so he invited the Candidate to come back to our offices to see me.

The Candidate was an Accountant, but also a bodybuilder (or at least he had the kind of physique that said, "I work out - look at me!") - I extended my hand to greet him and he crunched down on my fingers.

I saw stars, winched in pain, and just about cried - while he moved on, oblivious to the destruction he had just caused.

I came out of my funk just in time to see another Colleague of mine, who had witnessed my ordeal, nervously extend his hand to our visiting "Mr. Universe."

I don't know how that worked out for him, but at the time, I thought he would have been wise to have waited until I had rearranged my phalanges!

Once the introductions are over, you will be asked to sit down and the interview will start - usually with an ice-breaker, such as, "Tell us something about yourself."

Now, aren't you pleased you did all that homework that I asked you to do early on? Making sure that you really are your most important project.

Remember that this is just an ice-breaker, so the expectation is not that you give a 40 minute soliloquy; rather present a two minute synopsis of your education, background, and experience.

Then the Interviewer or members of the Panel will start to ask you various questions, most of which will fall under the broad topics previously covered.

Their agenda is to assess several things:

Most importantly; whether you will be a good corporate fit within their organizational culture. They want to see your personality. Are you deadly serious, do you have a sense of humor, are you quick witted and fun, or utterly humorless?

They really want to see whether you would fit in with the rest of their team, and if you are the kind of person, whom most other employees would want to work and also socialize with; this is an important aspect of doing business at the professional and executive level.

Your Leadership skills - depending on whether you will be running the Company, a division, or a department. They will question you about your Management and Leadership style.

Are you dictatorial and do you assert that others work for you, or is your style more collaborative, collegial, and inclusive?

Do you make your team feel that each person is strategic and important in their own right and that you are all working together for a common goal? They will want to know.

When answering questions, remember to speak in terms of "we" and not "I" - give lots of credit to your team, it gives the Interviewer and the Panel the impression that you are a team player, that you care about people, and aren't selfish!

Only answer in the first person if you are asked specifically, to state what *you* did.

Do you have in-depth industry experience and are you technically strong? This may or may not be important to the Company - but it is also something that you should be aware of prior to the interview. You will find out very quickly what criteria are most important to the Company for the particular role that you are filling.

Do you have the ability to be creative, innovative and think "outside the box"?

Are you a visionary? Can you take a Company to where it has never been before and build new markets, ideas, products, and services?

There are a myriad of questions that can be asked; however, at the senior level, you can expect these kinds of questions to come up.

Wendy's Melt Down

I do not coach Candidates on exactly the 101 or top 25 interview questions that you should definitely be able to answer, and there is a very good reason for this. I used to do this, until something happened that completely changed my thinking and the way I coach.

During the late 1990s, I was retained by a Client in the Not-for-Profit sector, an industry niche I seldom do work in, but the process of every Search Assignment is the same, irrespective of the industry.

I was asked to head-hunt a "Manager of Giving and Major Gifts." For those unsure of the meaning of that rather long and arduous title, it essentially means a Fund Raising Manager.

The search was progressing normally and to my delight, I found that there were many people well qualified and interested in the position, so getting a short-list of talented people was not difficult.

I interviewed one particular woman who, for the purposes of this story, I'll call Wendy.

Wendy was a good Candidate, certainly good enough to be short-listed. When she interviewed with me, she seemed fine; although she did allude to the fact that she had been out of the workforce, raising children, and had recently within the last year returned to work.

Prior to having children and electing to stay at home, she had worked for a charitable organization and had precisely the kind of experience that I was looking for.

At the time of our first meeting, I still had several Candidates to interview and did not know at that stage how she would measure up against the others. After completing my long-list interviews, I decided that Wendy was definitely a short-list Candidate.

I called her to tell her the good news, and she asked several question about what she could expect in terms of the kind of questions that could come up. I was more than happy to oblige her, did a good deal of coaching, and ultimately reassured her that she would be just fine!

What I did not know was that Wendy was either taking copious notes or else recording the conversation. A few days later, the Search Committee and I were all seated and ready to meet with the Candidates for their final interviews.

Wendy was not the first Candidate; she was the second. I went to fetch her at Reception and led her to our meeting room to meet the Committee, which included the Regional Manager in Vancouver, The Executive Director who had flown in from Toronto, and a few other Senior Professionals.

She seemed really nervous, more than I remembered her being when we first met. I bolstered her confidence by telling her that all would be fine - but she still looked so distraught, as if she was going in to hospital for emergency surgery.

I introduced her to the Panel and she was visibly shaken. I really could not understand why she was behaving so differently from when I saw her in person, so I thought it best to start with our usual "ice-breaker" to put her at ease and just get her talking. It always worked - on everyone!

"Wendy, all the members on the Panel have read my report on the Candidates, but why don't you tell us, in your own words, a little about yourself?" I asked amiably. I was also sitting closest to her, which I thought would give her added comfort and moral support.

Wendy looked at me as if she had seen a ghost. I repeated the question. She didn't say a word, the room went very still, and the atmosphere became extremely uncomfortable. Then she opened her jacket and from the front inside pocket retrieved a wad of notes. She carefully unfolded them and started to search for the question and began reading from her "crib notes!"

The Panel and I watched in stunned silence, mortified! I was so embarrassed.

Another member on the Panel followed up with a second question, so as to make an attempt to eliminate the long periods of silence - Wendy resorted back to her notes to try and find the appropriate answer to his question.

Then another person asked her a third question while Wendy yet again searched her notes for the best answer to the question. She made no eye contact with anyone - her response to each question was to hunt for the answer in her well scripted notes and robotically read what she had written.

It was excruciating to watch...and very humiliating for me. I had simply never seen anything like this in my life before, and I don't think anyone else in the room had either.

After the third question, I leaned towards her and gently took the wad of notes out of her hands. I thought she was going to faint.

"No-one is here to trick you or ask you any questions that you can't answer. We all believe in you and only want to get to know you better. So please, just answer the questions; you are more than capable of doing that," I reassured her.

She tried, but Wendy was a bundle of nerves, and I saw the Committee was in one accord; there was no way Wendy could ever be selected for the position - she could not cope with the slightest pressure. So, I did the only logical and rational thing left to do - bring the interview to a compassionate conclusion and walk her out of the room.

I thanked her for coming and said good bye. The Committee was extremely forgiving, as I re-entered the room more ashamed than I am able to articulate - they simply said in chorus; "Thank you!"

It was a pivotal moment for me - a lesson on how *not* to coach! I thought I was helping Wendy, but in truth, I was enabling her and doing her a great disservice. I realized that if a Candidate cannot handle the pressure of an interview, they will never be able to handle the challenges and demands of the job.

People have to be able to get a job on their own merit - so I now coach by helping people enhance their skills, tackle their fears head-on, and overcome whatever is holding them back.

In keeping with the ancient Chinese proverb: *I no longer feed people for a day, but teach them to fish for a life time.*

Teaching you to Ace one particular interview is not my objective - giving you the tools and guidance to Ace any interview is!

My desire is that every Candidate, after having gone through one of my coaching programs, is able to handle any interview question, no matter what is asked of them.

However, I also realize there are many of you that just want the "quick fix" i.e. just tell me what I have to say to the Interviewer so that I can get the job!

I have said previously that your Interviewer or Panel of Interviewers will be very sophisticated and experienced in conducting interviews. They know instinctively when a Candidate is trying to manipulate them, be evasive, or simply appease them by telling them what the *Candidate thinks the Interviewer wants to hear* - it will not work!

My advice is NOT to study clichéd questions and answers because you *will* come across as rehearsed, and nothing will destroy your chances of getting a job faster.

You have to be, do and know the following:

1. **Be Authentic:** You have to come across as authentic, and you are only capable of doing this if you truly are yourself. Your prospective employer is trying to find out who *you* are.

   They want to know if you are likeable, trustworthy, and genuine - these are the qualities that give you credibility. The virtues that establish whether you are someone that other people in the Company will want to work with.

2. **Be Kind and Respectful to everyone that you meet:**

   I cannot overstate this enough. It almost seems like such a redundant thing to emphasize, but I have seen arrogant Candidates, that were brilliant, lose the job because they were rude to the Receptionist.

   It happened to one of mine. It was a huge shock to him and enormously embarrassing to me. He was my top Candidate for the role. It was his opportunity to lose, and he did just that, by being rude and abusive to the Reception.

3. Know the following:

What you want in terms of the Company that you would like to work for. This includes industry, specific target Companies within that industry, and of course, the title and kind of job itself - you absolutely must know what kind of work you want to do.

Never be a "Jack of all trades" in the interview. It makes you look unfocused and unprepared. Remember, this is *your* career and your Interviewer will look to see how invested you are in your own career, how ambitious you are, how much thought, planning, and vision you put into what it is that you want to do.

You will almost always be asked what you are looking for, unless you have come through a retained Executive Search process, then these details would have been covered by the Search Consultant and the Company will have a detailed report on you.

However, be prepared for this question to *still* be asked, even if the above is true. Often, the Interviewer will want to see how congruent you are when speaking to them; versus what you told the Executive Search Consultant.

Everything that is in the Public Domain about the Company that you are interviewing with!

You have to look at their Corporate website and make note of the following:

- Exactly what they do, who their Competitors are, the Management Team, Board of Directors, recent Awards, Major Contracts, and also look to see if you know anyone in "The Executive."

- Their "Core Values" if these are published on their website. Are their Values congruent with yours?

- Recent News Releases; being current with what is happening to *them* shows that you are seriously interested, and this will bode well for you.

- Why you want to work for this particular Company? You will be asked, so have a well thought out answer *before* the interview.

- Why you want to leave your current employer. You will most certainly be asked this question.

My guidance here is the following:

1. Always make it about a progressive Career move for you. Never run down your current employer, boss, or colleague - even if your job situation is untenable.

2. The fact that you have to get out because you can't stand someone makes *you* look difficult and unprofessional!

3. Be as complimentary as you sincerely can be.

How to answer if you have been "let go" from your last job. This is possibly the most difficult question for someone who has just lost their job to answer.

Here are my guidelines for the different scenarios:

1. If you have been downsized because of a downturn in the economy or your industry, then this is not personal - so just tell them honestly what happened.

2. If the Company was good to you and you enjoyed working there, mention that too. It will show that you are not resentful about what happened and have moved on.

3. If you have been fired, and the Interviewer or someone on the Panel asks you outright if you were fired from your last position – you will have to answer this; it is not illegal, they are allowed to do so.

4. My advice is always be honest - I know this is difficult, but being sincere and honest shows your humanity and often the Interviewer or Panel will be more inclined to be empathetic towards you.

Most people at some stage in their careers have worked for impossible bosses - BUT never run anyone in the previous Company down (even if they jolly well deserve it!)

If you are asked what happened, within the guidelines of absolute honesty; **say something like the following:**

"The Board of Directors and I had a difference of opinion on where we felt the direction of the Company should go. They wanted to expand internationally and I felt that the timing wasn't right. We also never had the funds to fully support such an endeavor - so we agreed to part ways.

I loved the Company and it was certainly not what I wanted, but since leaving, I am more certain now that it was the best decision and I've decided to move forward.

I have a lot to offer and am looking forward to exploring the opportunities that are opening up for me!"

Always end with a positive statement on an upbeat tone!

Ask Questions and Take Notes

During the course of your Job Search Process, think of the questions that you would like to ask your Interviewer or members of the Panel. You should know ahead of time about the issues that are both important to you and pertinent to the Company, the industry it is in, and most especially, the position itself.

When you arrive and after you've been introduced, do ask if they mind, if you take notes. The Interviewer or Panel will most definitely say yes, but asking shows that you are considerate.

Jot down points on important issues as they come up. Clarify certain points of discussion while you are in the interview - this will give you a reference point later on when you may wish to come back to certain things that were discussed and also when you wish to mention these talking points in your "Thank You" note.

Keep your notes brief - you do not want to miss the opportunity to look at your Interviewer, nor do you want to break eye contact to such an extent that all they see is you bending down over your notebook and writing copiously.

There is no alternative for looking at someone and allowing them the same curtesy. It allows them to size you up, evaluate you, and see how you handle pressure. More importantly, it also gives both you and your Interviewer an opportunity to build rapport - that's why there is simply no substitute for a face-to-face interview.

Appropriate Behavior In An Interview

I don't know what it is about interviews that make some Candidates shine and others act crazy!

Actually, let me re-think and reword that. The Candidates that shine are usually the ones that take my advice, and those that act crazy are the ones, that generally think they don't need to, and then it all plays out in the interview...

Interviews, especially the Panel ones are the great levelers because the Panel sees all the Candidates on the same day, and the Candidates are generally asked the same questions. The playing field is about as level as it can get - so this type of interview is completely fair and as equitable as it can possibly be.

A member of the Panel may dig deeper with a particular Candidate if they are interested in what that person did and think that it may be valuable to the Company, but this in no way skews the process or introduces bias.

Several years ago, I was retained by a big Company to headhunt a Chief Information Officer for them. The Company was a major employer in the town and many people that lived in this small city had, at some stage, either worked for the Corporation or at least interviewed for a position with them.

My Candidates were drawn from a pool of national Candidates. The Company was a desirable place to work, enjoyed a high profile, and was well known nationally, so there was no shortage of interest in the position.

I interviewed several Candidates, and there were a few local Candidates. The short-list was culled down from many to about five Candidates: one local and four from out of town.

The local Candidate, Wendell, was clearly very keen on the position. I asked him if he had interviewed with the Company before; he said he hadn't, but mentioned immediately that he knew they were looking and thought he would be a good fit.

I thought he was worth short-listing. Wendell knew the Company well and that can be an advantage, but I knew that he would have very stiff competition. I also wanted to see what the CEO's preference was. Would he prefer a local guy or someone from out of town? I did not know which way he was leaning.

Anyway, the day of the short-list interviews arrived, and the Company decided that they wanted to have the interviews at one of the lovely hotels in the city.

I always try and do what is best for the Candidates, so I let them decide when they want to be interviewed: first, last or somewhere in between. Wendell elected to go first.

The conference room was set up as a fairly large Boardroom with a big screen in front for the Presentation that each Candidate was asked to prepare.

I, as the Facilitator, was seated nearest to the door so that I could go and collect the Candidates when they were ready, bring them into the room, introduce them to the Panel, and then walk them out after the interview.

There was the designated "hot seat" for the Candidate at the head of the table, and the rest of the Panel sat wherever it suited them on both sides of the table.

I entered the room with Wendell, and everyone greeted him warmly; the CEO announced that he had just arrived in time for breakfast!

Breakfast was arranged buffet style on another table against the wall. Wendell wasted no time helping himself; in fact, he looked rather eager. He was a big guy and obviously enjoyed his food.

I decided that I had too much to worry about, so I just poured some orange juice in a wine glass, (the only glasses available) and sat down to quickly go through some final notes. Wendell asked where he should sit and we all pointed to the "hot seat" that was a few feet away from where I was sitting; we all had plenty of room.

After a sumptuous breakfast, it was time for Wendell's presentation.

He rose from the "hot seat" came over to my side to better stand on the opposite side to the CEO and in full view of the Panel. He was well positioned to take charge of the room and own it, he certainly did!

He pranced around and then would stop suddenly (talking and prancing) to make sure that he had the undivided attention of the whole room, paused for effect, and then started up again. It was really most peculiar.

Then to my surprise and shock really, when he was asked, "Tell us something about yourself," Wendell proudly announced that he was from (and he mentioned the specific town, a really small town a few miles away from the city in which we were interviewing) and then he further reassured everyone that he was "here to stay!"

What possessed him to say that? Surely, when you haven't been a mile from the cow shed - why mention it! Most of the other Candidates were well travelled, and the Candidate that ultimately got the job had international experience, as well.

It is always an advantage to have international experience on one's Resume; it shows that one is ambitious, open to diversity, and willing to travel, which broadens one's knowledge.

I watched the CEO - he did not take his eyes off Wendell. I was wondering what he was thinking, but also thirsty by now; I reached out my hand to the right where my orange juice was - there was nothing! I thought to myself, "That's impossible; I remember putting the glass on my right hand side, for easy reach and retrieval. Where was my darn orange juice?"

I looked around, thinking I may have forgotten it on the buffet table - no, it wasn't there. Then I looked up at Wendell who had taken command of the room and was swigging something down - my orange juice!

I got the giggles, but suppressed it. Anyone who knows me knows that I love to laugh and cannot stop when I get started, so best not to get started - this was not the forum. To make matters worse, no-one seemed to notice, not even Wendell, who was now oblivious to what he had done and was knocking his head back to drain the last drop - there goes my orange juice!!!

The CEO seemed mesmerized by him. Was this a good thing? I could not get any sense as to whether he was mortified by his performance or impressed. I would hate to play poker with these guys; they were so good at controlling their emotions.

Wendell was still standing, looking ever so debonair, with glass in one hand (the remnants of my orange juice) and clicker for his presentation in the other.

He moved towards the table to put down the glass and then realized what he had done, "Oh, it's yours! Do you want it back?" No! I didn't, and shook my head slightly; enough for him to read my response.

Gosh! I could not wait for this interview to be over…and eventually it was. The Panel thanked him for coming, and I walked him out the door towards the elevators. Wendell, smug as ever, said, "I think that went well!" It was one of those few occasions when I was lost for words, but I thanked him for coming and promised to get back to him.

I really needed to have a quiet moment to just "laugh it out." After that, I returned, a lot more composed to the room just in time to hear the CEO talking about Wendell.

Never mind the loss of my orange juice, the real clanger was about to hit! - And this one wasn't so funny… The CEO turned to me and said, "I saw him five years ago, and he was better then!"

It's never good to find out these kinds of surprises from a Client. I should have known that, and to find out that he had actually *regressed*? This was awful. Wendell was not only an orange juice thief; he was a liar too…

People do silly things in an interview. What upset me the most was that it looked as if I had not adequately prepared in finding out that my Candidate had been interviewed by the Client before.
There was nothing wrong in him reapplying, but I should have known this information. I would have notified the Client that he wanted to reapply and asked if they had any objection to seeing him again.

Wendell had other plans for me though. He thought that if he lied by omission, I would not find out. However, because of his aberrant behavior, arrogant stance, and other antics, the CEO could not wait to tell me.

Lesson learned; I never referred Wendell to another Client again!

© Randy Glasbergen / glasbergen.com

**"I suffer from post-traumatic stress disorder.
Not from the war, from my last job interview."**

Action Steps

1. Think about how badly you want this position and how hard you have worked to get to this point - don't take unnecessary risks that could cost you the opportunity.

2. Never underestimate the competition or the ability of the Interviewer or Panel to throw a curveball at you in terms of a question that you never expected - it happens all the time.

   That's why all the preparation leading up to this point is absolutely critical.

   Take every day that you have at your disposal to prepare to deliver your best effort - don't squander the time; the competition is always stiffer than you think.

   Do what you need to do to maintain a high level of interest and energy throughout the period of the job search so that you can prepare to best advantage.

3. Be strategic, stay focused, look after your health, exercise and pace yourself - you may need to maintain your physical stamina, emotional well-being, and mental acuity for a prolonged period of time.

   Take the preparation as seriously as you can. You cannot slack off or lower your guard.

   Nothing is a done deal until you have a contract that is signed, sealed, and delivered - with your name on it!

CHAPTER 8

What *You* Need To Do
After The Interview -
The Proper Protocol
For Candidates

*"No duty is more urgent than
that of returning thanks!"*

James Allen

When it comes to Candidates - there are two kinds of Candidates that we remember. The first kind are those that are civil, grateful, and appreciative, who demonstrate their feelings by saying "Thank You."

The second kind are those that are rude and ill-bred. Not saying "Thank You" is a sign of being ill-bred. Being too lazy or tardy can not only cost you the job, but worse it can cost you the relationship with the person who interviewed you!

According to research, 75% of Hiring Managers say that receiving a "Thank You" note affects their hiring decision - so if this is news to you, all I can say is the person or people who interviewed you are *expecting* your "Thank You" note!

There is also specific protocol to adhere to when it comes to "Thank You" notes, such as timing, content, appropriate comments, what never to say, and always check for errors.

Thank You Notes

When to Send them

Normal dictates say within 24 hours, so that things are still fresh in your mind and you in the Interviewer's mind. I agree that sooner is definitely better, but within 48 hours is still perfectly acceptable. What I don't want, however, is for you to just rush off a scripted email with little thought and plenty of errors. That being said, I don't want you to wait longer than 48 hours either.

Remember the "Thank You" note goes so much further than simply thanking the Interviewer for his or her time. It is another opportunity to reaffirm that you are a great Candidate and should be seriously considered for a multitude of reasons!

Your immediate task before even drafting that "Thank You" note is to sit down and do a thorough post-mortem of the interview, review the good things that reassured you that you were doing well and the questions you wished you had answered differently.

Then draft the "Thank You" note and once again, just like you did after your Phone or Skype interview (if you had them), discuss the outcome and how you felt the interview went with a trusted friend or advisor.

Listen to their advice and make the suggested edits as you see fit. The tone and content of the note, still has to be in your "voice" and be congruent with how you feel about the Company, your fit within the Company, the job itself, and how you believe you can contribute.

What to Send - Email or Handwritten?

People are always in a dilemma as to what is most appropriate. My advice is the following:

- If you've had a Phone or Skype Interview - then an email is perfectly acceptable.

- With a Face-to-Face Interview - You should send both. Once you know what you want to say and have gone through my suggestions above, send an email as soon as possible and a brief handwritten note as well.

People so seldom get a handwritten note, which makes them appreciated all the more. It also takes more effort to do this, and I want you to be seen as someone who goes the extra mile. Super achievers make the effort that losers scoff at.

Why both? The handwritten note will make you look more polished, show that you make the effort to do things properly, and above all, it reinforces who you are to the Interviewer. You do not know how many people your Interviewer, or Panel, is seeing for this particular position. You absolutely want to stand out!

The email will provide you with the opportunity to say more than you could possibly in the handwritten note. The handwritten note is, by design, meant to be short. Just thank the Interviewer and restate your desire to help them succeed in whatever endeavor or challenge the Company may be facing. That's it!

Personalize the Note

You must get the name of the person who interviewed you, and if you were seen by a Panel, then it is imperative that you ask for all their business cards before you leave the interview.

This will ensure that:

- You get everyone's name correct and
- You are able to personalize each email and handwritten note.

You will only be able to personalize a note if you have concentrated and been fully present in the interview, taken appropriate notes, and done a post-mortem after the interview.

I cannot overstate the importance of this - you never want to make mistakes and mention something in an email that was never attributed to that person, but rather someone else.

Please, if you have had a Panel interview - do not send everyone the same note. People often read out their notes aloud - trust me, I've been in the room when that happens. Another Panel member will laugh and say, "Gosh! Sounds exactly like mine!"

Don't squander an opportunity to look good by doing something foolish. Make the time to remember what was important to each Panel member, and address that separately to them in personalized emails.

Reference Talking Points, Issues, and Challenges

You will need to refer to your notes for these; that's why it is imperative to take notes during the interview, and write down what you remember after the interview when you are alone. This is part of your analysis of how the interview went.

Further discuss these talking points, issues, and challenges with your trusted friend or advisor and seek their opinion and counsel. Mention how you would like to address each in emails and hear their advice. After your session with your advisor - sit down and draft that email, or several depending on the number of people you saw.

Remember, your emails should be in "your voice" and your Interviewers should be able to reconfirm in their minds that what you are saying is congruent with the responses that you gave in your interview.

Reaffirm Your Interest and Commitment to Helping the Company Achieve Its Goals

Leave your Interviewer or members of the Panel with the impression that you are interested; that your education, background and industry experience would be a good fit for the Position and that you as a person, would be an Asset to the Company, and most importantly that you have the necessary expertise to help them with their challenges.

In essence, let them know that you are able to contribute immediately! This will confirm for them that you *are* the best person for the job!

End Off by Thanking the Interviewer Again

Sign off your email by thanking your Interviewer once more and let them know that you are keenly looking forward to hearing back from them with regards to the next steps in the process.

Never plead and beg for more time - you don't want to look desperate, but rather strong and independent. Remember, *you* are the prize here, and your expertise and past successes make you highly marketable!

What Never to Say in a Thank You Note

1. Don't ever mention Salary - this is not the time or place, and you have no idea how they really feel about you; there is still a long way to go in the process.

2. Never squander the opportunity to make an additional good impression by telling your Interviewer what *you* want or ask for something. This is not the time to say how much you enjoyed the interview, but if you don't get the job - could the Interviewer please refer you to someone else who may be looking to hire.

3. Make sure that your "Thank You" note has been vetted for appropriate language and content. Your message should always be consistent and in agreement with the impression they got of you in the interview. Don't forget to spell the Interviewer's name correctly.

4. Never say anything disparaging about yourself or anyone else. Your note should always end on an upbeat tone and give the impression that you are keen to move forward and have something substantial to contribute to their organization!

What Not To Do

Nesbert was a Candidate of mine who had a good interview, and immediately afterwards, set about writing his handwritten "Thank You" notes.

He did not do a post-mortem of the interview, as I have suggested one do; but rather was in a "dead heat" rush to get his "Thank

You" notes to the Panel that had just interviewed him barely thirty minutes before!

Nobody knew that he was going to do this - least of all me. So what happened? Well, after we said goodbye to Nesbert, he was led to the elevator, and a few minutes later, the next Candidate was received and walked to the Boardroom to meet with the Panel.

We had just finished the introductions to the Panel, and my Candidate was doing his Presentation to the Committee. He was an excellent Candidate in the midst of doing a fine Presentation. I could see that the Panel was most impressed.

He was really smart, energetic, engaging, and so interesting to listen to. All of a sudden, the door opened and someone entered to deliver several white envelopes that were handed to the Panel.

I did not receive one, but I watched as each member of the Panel opened their envelope, curious to see what it was, not knowing if it was something urgent.

Judging from their faces, I realized immediately what they were; "Thank You" notes - Nesbert's!

He must have felt smug with himself for getting his "Thank You" notes in before anyone else - but there was something even more insidious. I could not help thinking that the timing was deliberate.

He knew that people instinctively would open an envelope handed to them, and if he handed them in right now, then he would interrupt the presentation that the current Candidate was giving, which is exactly what happened!

All eyes turned to open and read what had been handed to them, and the Panel stopped listening to my Candidate. Now this only took a few minutes, but it left me boiling.

It is mean-spirited to go out of your way to deliberately and purposefully sabotage someone else! If you think this is a good strategy for getting ahead, by undermining someone else, then I'd rather we did not meet.

In a cruel twist of fate, Nesbert actually landed the job - but Karma was waiting for him, he did not cope very well and struggled to hang on to it…

By rushing to get his "Thank You" notes to the Interview Committee - he never took the time to personalize them. He could not have done so, as there simply wasn't the time to do it.

So, they must all have been generic. There was no way he could have addressed the specific issues that arose in the department in which Nesbert would eventually work.

He never bothered to address the challenges the company was facing or how he would solve them, were he to get the position - so please learn from this story. What Nesbert did, was wrong on so many levels.

Additional Commentary on the Importance of Simply Saying "Thank You"

A friend of mine recently called me to tell me of an event that had happened to her. She got a call from a former colleague to ask if my friend would meet her for lunch. The colleague mentioned to my friend that she was desperately looking for work and had noted that despite the economy being down, my friend has always managed to land on her feet and find work.

My friend was pleased to be of help. She is a kind, generous person and has many friends because of her disposition and professionalism. To preface this story, both women are professionals and work in an industry where their skills are highly sought after; despite that, the industry in which they worked was very dependent on one particular market sector - which was in a free fall. This resulted in many people in that sector being out of work.

The two ladies met for lunch, and my friend explained that part of her "good fortune" in always being employed was that she kept up her contacts, in good times and bad, and was always helpful in whatever way she could be. She stressed to her colleague that one must be open to giving if you want others to be there for you when you need them.

My friend was explaining to her colleague that when you invite someone out for lunch with the objective of getting referrals or "picking their" brain or with the intention of simply getting something out of the meeting - then *you* (meaning the person who suggested the meeting and solicited the other) should be the *one* to pay for the meal.

The colleague listened intently, and then came straight to the point, "Would you ask your boss whether there is any chance that there might be work for me with his Company?"
"Sure I will," said my friend.

The ladies continued talking and at the end of the "lunch date" - requested by the colleague, the waiter placed the bill on their table. The colleague reached for the bill and said, "Well then! Shall we each pay for ourselves?" and proceeded to *only* pay for *herself!*

She seemed completely oblivious to the message! How incredibly self-serving; but there was more to come...

My friend had promised that she would speak to her boss on behalf of her colleague, and true to her word, she did just that. My friend spoke to her boss right away, on return to her office, and asked her boss whether there was an opportunity at the Company for her former colleague.

As it turned out, my friend's boss knew her former colleague very well. There had been a time when the market for their skills had been very buoyant and the demand far outweighed the availability for people with this particular skill set.

My friend's boss had, unbeknown to my friend, called her former colleague a few years prior and asked the colleague whether she would be interested in working for his Company. The colleague at the time was gainfully employed and was very rude to the boss. She practically put the phone down on him as he was bothering her, and she was clearly not interested!

The memory was crystal clear in his mind. Because of the ill-mannered, brusque way she spoke to him and her bad attitude, he made a decision that he would never call her again.

So, with regards to offering her employment now - when *she* needed a job? Well, it would be fair to say that he was not even prepared to consider her!

Of course, the colleague had *never* mentioned this to my friend.

I have many similar stories of Candidates who only take and never give back. They have an expectation that one is there to serve them. A sense of entitlement that their needs should be uppermost on my mind and a personal priority for me.

One such Candidate was a lawyer who was referred to me by a very nice Candidate that was already on my database. As the source of the referral was a trusted person, my assumption was that the referred Candidate would be a very nice person as well. I could not have been more wrong! Of course, I would only know that with hindsight...

The referred Candidate was a highly priced lawyer earning well into six figures, and for once in his life, found himself in transition. He was from the East Coast, but decided that he would broaden his search. The two cities he was prepared to consider working and living in were Toronto and Vancouver.

He contacted me on an unsolicited basis, which means that I did not have any position for him and would have to clear my very busy schedule to accommodate him. I was also living in the United States by then, and he would be visiting Vancouver in Canada, so I would not only have to make time to see him (without any solid reason), but I'd also have to travel across the border into another country to meet with him. This would be entirely all on my time and at my expense.

His expectations just escalated from there. The only day that he could see me was on a Public Holiday. I saw that there was no compromise on any front from his side, so I ought to just have said, "No!" Of course, the original referral was a really nice guy, and I did not want to let him down - so I acquiesced.

As it was a Public Holiday - my office building was closed; no elevators were working. I did find this out beforehand, and set up a time to have lunch at a fine restaurant at one of the top hotels.

What I did not expect, however, was that the elevators from the Parkade within the hotel were also not working. I ended up walking up about eight floors to eventually get into the lobby of the hotel. I was not a happy camper at this stage...

I made my way to the restaurant, and he was already there waiting for me. Trying to make light of what had happened, I told him the elevators in the hotel parking were also shut off - he looked at me with complete indifference. The only concern he had was ordering his meal.

We spoke and I did a detailed interview with him, at the end of which I told him that I have a unique way of coaching my Candidates that yields incredible results. I did stress that it was a collaborative effort and that if he wanted to work with me, it would require a commitment of time on his part. He could not have been more disinterested if he tried.

Eventually, we finished the meal and the interview - the waiter brought the bill and placed it before him. He did not move a muscle to pay - so I dutifully paid. I thought that he might at least say, "Thank you," - but it never came.

As he was in transition and told me that he needed a job fairly urgently, I suggested that we start coaching the following Monday.

I told him that as soon as I got home, I would email him several assignments that I'd require him to do over the following week. He looked at me with absolute disgust and contempt, "Oh no," he said, "we can't start next Monday - that's a Public Holiday in Ontario, and I'm spending time with *my* family!"

I was mortified, and then it hit me. I was more invested in his success than he was. I politely said goodbye and thought I would wait to hear from him to see when it would be more convenient for him.

Well, I never heard from him after that. There was no follow up "Thank You for Seeing Me" email or, in fact, any communication whatsoever until several months later when he remembered that I was coming to Toronto for a big conference. I got an email from him that simply read, "If you want to see me, let me know."

Really? I neither needed nor wanted to see him - so, I deleted him from my database.

People who are selfish and self-serving may score some time or advantage in the beginning of a relationship, but they lose out in the long term. Remember what I wrote about in Chapter Three - Changing the Paradigm from Getting to Giving.

The Universe works on an intrinsic law of "reciprocity" - a "quid pro quo" basis if you will - which makes life fair and equitable for all. When selfishness is allowed to creep into a relationship and disturb that delicate balance - it kills the relationship!

Action Steps

1. If you want to be remembered for your good manners - show other people that you have them.

2. You will be judged, not on your good intentions, but what you actually do! So write the "Thank You" note, and always remember to treat others as you would like them to treat you.

3. Not acknowledging a kind deed or remembering to say "Thank you" will cost you enormously in the future.

CHAPTER 9

What to Expect After
The Final Interview

*"Patience is Power. Patience is not an absence of action;
rather it is "timing". It waits on the right time to act,
for the right principles and in the right way."*

Fulton J. Sheen

As mentioned previously, the "final" interview is not
necessarily the final interview - it depends entirely on whether
you are having a one-on-one meeting with an HR Manager or
other senior representative from the Company; this will be based
on the Company's hiring policy.

Being interviewed with only one person present tends to happen
when you have approached the Company directly on your own or
been referred through a recruitment agency, and in some instances
even through a Headhunter.

My preference is always the Panel interview, which is more
common at the executive level. In our industry, the day that all

Candidates meet the Panel is referred to as the day for final interviews.

I will come back to what happens if you've been interviewed by a Panel; for now, let's just discuss what happens after your one-on-one interview with just a single Interviewer.

When the interview ends, do thank the Interviewer for their time and ask what the next steps are. Do not leave without asking - especially if you have approached the Company on your own as you have no-one to contact afterwards, such as a Headhunter or recruiter to ask what the feedback was and what the next steps in the search process are.

It is also perfectly in order for you to ask your Interviewer whether they mind if you follow up with them. I prefer this approach to simply waiting to hear back. You will also feel more in control if there is some task that is within your power.

Never discuss salary at your first meeting; this is inappropriate as no-one will make a decision after seeing you once. The Company is a long way off from making an offer to anyone at this stage - you included. It is safe to assume that there will be several Candidates that are being interviewed for this position.

Don't ask the Interviewer for feedback on your performance in the interview - this is equally inappropriate, it makes you look needy and insecure, and it puts your Interviewer on the spot, which will make them uncomfortable.

Even if your interview went well and you get the distinct feeling that you built great rapport with your Interviewer - that person will still want to discuss their impression of you with other senior people in the Company.

Very few people ever make a hiring decision on their own, based on only one interview - unless they are a very small Company and you are interviewing directly with the owner and founder of the Company.

If you've had a face-to-face interview with one particular Interviewer from the Company's side and it went well - you may, in all probability, be contacted again to meet with several more senior people who are responsible for hiring, including the senior person that you will be reporting to.

The question, however, is what do you do in the meantime while you are waiting to hear back?

The first thing you need to do is your follow up "Thank You" note we discussed earlier. That's your first priority.

Then get a list of references ready. There is specific protocol with regards to references, what kind, how many etc. - we will cover all of them in due course.

If you were referred by an Executive Headhunter and were one of the Candidates on a Panel interview, your Executive Search Consultant will be responsible for taking care of issues like the next steps and getting back to you with constructive feedback.

As an Executive Search Consultant, I'm a facilitator on the Panel, which means that essentially my responsibility is to make sure that the day goes smoothly and without a hitch. I also guide the Panel from the one Candidate to the next, ensuring that every Candidate gets the same treatment and amount of time with the Panel.

We have a standard set of questions which all Candidates are asked. At the end of the day, the Search Committee debriefs and rates each of the Candidates against a matrix that lists the most important criteria for the position.

The criteria usually comprise key attributes deemed essential to the role which have been pre-determined by the Search Committee. Fundamental key attributes would be considered to be characteristics, such as leadership ability, cultural fit, industry experience, etc.

The Search Committee is made up of Senior Executives who will be dealing primarily with the Candidate and often working closely with the Candidate once they have been hired.

So, once the Committee has concluded their debriefing session at the end of the day - generally, one or two Candidates emerge as the top two favorites, based on how well they rated against the key criteria in the matrix.

Sometimes there is one clear "winner" - but if the search is well done, most of the time, there usually are at least two Candidates that rise to the top, as the competition is fierce. Of course, the objective of the Executive Headhunter is always to deliver the best people on the market to the Client.

The Executive Headhunter will then be responsible for getting back to all Candidates with feedback and the top Candidate or two will inevitably be invited back to the Company to meet more Senior People and often additional important Stakeholders or even Members of the Board.

What all Candidates should do is have a ready list of references, especially if you are in transition and pro-actively looking for a new position. In fact, if you were to be interviewed by me - I would certainly have been discussing this with you at our initial meeting.

I like being prepared and never wait this far into the process to run references unless there is a very specific reason to hold off. Very rarely do I submit a Candidate for a search unless I have already referenced them. I hate surprises, and the kind of surprises one finds out under these circumstances is inevitably bad.

Whatever the timing of the references, you will be asked for them, so you might as well do them sooner, rather than later and get the best references that you can. Once again, it always comes down to careful preparation and planning.

References

Firstly, I cannot stress enough how critically important it is to have a good list of references. It is almost impossible to get a position without the hiring Company doing two specific things:

1. Running References and
2. Doing Pre-Employment Checks

The Company hiring a Candidate is investing a large sum of money, especially if they have used a Retained Headhunter. Notwithstanding the initial cost of an Executive Search, there are much larger costs, such as the Candidates Full Salary Package and additional costs, like Severance Pay, if that Candidate does not work out.

Should the Candidate not work out, the cost to the Company can often be as high as a full year's salary, and I have even seen Companies liable for more than double that, so no-one wants to make a mistake. In addition to the costs mentioned, there is also the cost of loss of morale to the company and lost credibility and reputation to the Headhunter - one simply cannot put a price on that.

So, what do we do to mitigate the risk of a bad hire? We do thorough screening at the initial interviews and beyond, run references, and do pre-employment checks.

With the advent of technology and the Internet, there are people who are buying their degrees from "Paper Mills."

"Paper Mills" are fictitious Companies registered by crooks that are just too happy to print Degrees and Certificates and sell them to very willing buyers, who then pass them off as real Degrees, when they are in fact, fake!

If you think I am making this up - I can assure you I am not kidding at all!

I learned all this first hand when I was doing Pre-Employment checks on Candidates of mine. I discovered two Candidates who had done this, and neither was even remotely worried that they might be caught as no-one had ever checked their credentials before I did - now I check everyone *before* I ever submit their Candidacy....

Criteria To Consider When Drawing Up A List Of References

1. Select Your References Carefully

The people who are going to be your references should be your advocates. People who know you well and can speak to your work experience, strengths, achievements, and leadership skills - so please give due consideration to who would do you justice and speak well of your accomplishments.

These references should be a good mix of people that you have either worked with or done business with. Your list should include "360 degree" References, meaning Superiors, Colleagues, Subordinates, and Clients (these can be Internal as well as External).

Please note there should be no Personal References on your List or "Character References." Your Professional References will be able to speak to your character.

© Randy Glasbergen / glasbergen.com

"Allen is an incredibly wonderful, generous, exciting, fun, kind, loving, brilliant, very special human being. This personal reference from your dog is quite impressive."

2. Contact Your References Directly

There is a certain protocol to remember when dealing with references.

If you are in close contact with a particular person on your reference list and they know that you are in transition and pro-actively looking for work, it is fine to contact them via email.

If you wish to use a certain person as a reference, but have not seen them for a long time; it is best to call and ask to see them directly - better still, take them out for lunch. They will be more empathetic and understanding with regards to your situation, and once again, nothing is more preferable than a one-on-one meeting.

First ask your contact whether they mind being a reference for you. They will inevitably say yes! Then thank them and tell them that you sincerely appreciate that.

Always show that you are grateful - no relationship should ever be taken for granted, and you never know when you might need them again.

Then let them know which Recruiters or Headhunters may be calling them - give your reference all the names of the people you are working with as well as their full contact information.

If, in addition to the aforementioned, you are also conducting some independent activities on your own - let them know what companies you have approached, who you have seen, and let your reference know who they can expect to get a call from.

Make sure your reference is well informed - remember no-one likes to be caught off guard. Ensure that your reference has your latest updated Resume and Cover Letter.

You, in turn, need to ensure that you have your reference's latest updated contact information so that the information on your list of references is current. Nothing is more frustrating than having a deadline and trying to contact references only to find out at the eleventh hour that their information is wrong...

Finally after lunch, or if you have heard back from them via email confirming that they are happy to provide a reference for you, follow up with a "Thank You" email.

3. How Many To Include? - More Is Better

I like to ask for at least six references. This may sound like a lot, but if you follow the 360 degree rule, and it is by no means cast in stone, merely a guideline, then you have one reference only from each type of person - i.e. Superior, Colleague, Subordinate, and Client.

The supplementary two references I'd like from two additional Superiors since they are in the best position to speak to your accomplishments; their opinion will always carry the most weight!

4. Why Letters Of Recommendation Are Valueless

You are able to personally read every word that has been written about you - it is hardly a confidential document or an objective citation of your accomplishments.

Whoever gave you the reference will inevitably say only nice things about you, rendering the opinion worthless.

Employers and other Third Parties, such as Headhunters, like to be able to speak directly to your references and be able to ask them specific things about you that might never be disclosed in an open document. That is why we refer to references as being confidential!

© Randy Glasbergen / glasbergen.com

"I'm pleased with the results of your drug test. We found traces of greed, tenacity and ambition in your urine!"

Pre-Employment Checks

With the increase in White Collar Crime - more and more Employers seek to mitigate the risk of hiring a Senior Professional who may not be who they pretend to be. People freely embellish their Resumes and present fake degrees. As most Senior Executives are in a fiduciary capacity to the Company - this puts the Company in a very vulnerable position.

So understandably, Companies are using every tool available to ensure that their next Senior Hire is not a criminal. From a Candidate's perspective - expect that this is going to become the norm.

In today's world, you will first be screened out via Social Media. If you make it through the first set of scrutiny, then you'll face the in-depth interview, probably with a Panel or multiple one-on-one interviews with several Senior Officials.

Get through that, then an HR Manager or the Headhunter will run references on you and finally, you'll be checked generally through an Independent Firm for any misdemeanors that you might have "forgotten" to mention - The latter being Pre-Employment Checks.

For the Pre-Employment Checks, you will be asked for Photo ID and your Social Insurance Number (SIN) for Canada or your Social Security Number (SSN) for the USA.

There really is no preparation that you can do for this except to be completely honest with the first person who interviews you, should there be something in your background you'd rather no-one knew about.

Pre-Employment Checks generally cover the following, although an Employer may ask for additional checks to be run.

- Criminal Conviction Records Search
- Credit Report
- Motor Vehicle Records
- Education Verification
- Bankruptcy Search
- Drug Test

The Importance of Being Honest

According to National Geographic, a great white shark can detect one drop of blood in 25 gallons (100 litres) of water and can sense even tiny amounts of blood up to 3 miles (5 kilometers) away.

I am like that when I hear someone lie. I have alarm bells going off in my head! In addition, my BS Meter is finely tuned to "hypersensitive."

Several years ago, I was retained by a start-up Company in the resource sector. My direct contact was the CEO of the Company, a really nice man who was professional, kind, and gentle.

He spoke to me about hiring their first Chief Financial Officer (CFO) - which I was glad to do. The search went well, and the Candidates were very good. This was a highly desirable position, and the remuneration was generous.

I found all the Candidates cooperative, except for one - Kent!

He would not provide references; I had no trouble in this regard from any of the other Candidates. I asked Kent repeatedly, and eventually told him that I could not present his candidacy if I could not reference check him.

He became absolutely belligerent. In one of his particularly bad episodes, he had a full blown screaming match with me, which ended up with him slamming the phone down.

I did not call him back, but shortly thereafter, I received a call from the CEO who called to tell me that Kent phoned him to apologize (to the CEO - not for the way he had spoken to me!) and explained to the CEO that he would no longer be dealing with me, but rather with the CEO directly!

I was furious, but had to stifle my feelings. It was an awful situation, but curiously idiotic, in that I had, on one side, an easy, kind (and way too understanding) Client and on the other side, a Candidate from hell - who had in essence cut me out of my own search process!

Naturally I was upset, but I was more humiliated that the search had gotten out of control, and now the Candidate was in the driver's seat.

I spoke to the CEO privately; he tried to reassure me that it was OK with him, and asked me to allow Kent to be interviewed. The CEO said, "Let's see him together with the other Candidates, and if we like him, do the references afterwards if that is a sticking point with him."

The Client dictates the mandate, and I dutifully went along with the CEO's suggestion. I privately met with the Search Committee for the Company, made up of other Senior Executives and Board

Members, and we decided on a day that was mutually convenient for the Panel interviews.

The Candidates presented one after the other. There was one super Candidate who we all knew was in a league of his own, but we also realized that he was highly marketable and would be more expensive. He also probably had more offers to choose from - which turned out to be exactly true, so the Panel turned to their next Candidate of choice - Kent!

Ah - yes! - Dear Kent, who presented very well and thoroughly impressed the Search Committee with his guile and cunning!

I was still steaming from the way I had been treated, and could barely look at him as he cleverly avoided all contact with me. During the debriefing after the interviews, it soon became clear that the top Candidate was outside of the Client's budget, so Kent by default became the Candidate of choice. I was not overly worried because I realized that the Client would never make him an offer before I had a chance to run references - but this was going to turn out to be way harder than I ever imagined…

The next day, I called all the Candidates and determined to be professional - I called Kent too (it was my duty). I let him know that, he was the Committee's choice, and naturally he was delighted. I again asked for his references. He said nothing, but I thought I would give him the benefit of the doubt and wait a day or two before pushing for them again.

Two nights later, I woke up in a cold sweat! It had to do with the search, and of course, it had to do with Kent! Something was terribly wrong, and I just had to speak to the CEO, who I had now not spoken to for a few days as he had been busy in meetings.

I could hardly wait for the morning - and I called the CEO as soon as I could. His secretary told me that he was tied up in meetings the whole day - but I simply *had t*o see him - so I rushed to his office, unannounced, and without an appointment.

A short while later, he came out of one meeting and saw me in the reception area - he smiled broadly and seemed really pleased to see me, "I was thinking of you today," he said, "I was just about ready to email Kent his letter of offer! Come to my office and I will show it to you," he said.

I was ready to pass out - "That's why I'm here!" I said, "I don't *want* you to send it off!"

"Why not?" asked the puzzled CEO.

"I haven't been able to run references on him yet, and I believe something is terribly wrong - I don't know what because I have not been given a chance to find out - but something is terribly wrong!"

He smiled reassuringly, "Don't worry," he said, "I've worked with difficult people before - I know how to handle him."

"That's not what I mean," I protested, "something is off - I don't know what, but I am determined to find out. Until such time, *please* don't send him the offer!"

"I have to Leora, I spoke to Kent this morning and told him that I would send him his offer in an hour or so, and that time is long past - so I have to send it!"

"Well, we can change the offer. We can add a contingency clause stating that the offer is contingent on his references being favorable - *Please* would you do that for me?" By now I was pleading...

"Of course, I will," he said; "If it will make you feel better - we'll do it right away." Together, we drafted the contingency clause and redid the letter of offer. I was so grateful to have such an understanding Client - a wave of absolute peace came over me. I asked for a copy and left his office with it in hand.

Walking back to my office, I reflected on what had just happened. If I had to tell any of my peers that I had just talked a Client of mine *out* of hiring a Candidate that they wanted - they would think I was absolutely crazy!

Any other Headhunter would have been thrilled that both parties wanted the deal and would have simply gone with the flow, collected the final retainer, and moved on to the next assignment.

However, I am not "any other Headhunter"…I am me, and I simply could not ignore the warning signs that were going off, even though this decision would cost me greatly. If my gut feeling was right, I would have to go back to the drawing board and redo the entire search all over again at my own cost.

I also wondered what the CEO thought of me - did he think I was nuts? I'm sure being talked *out of* hiring a Candidate was a first for him too…

The next day, I received the following email from my Client:

"I just wanted to pass on the encouragement and support from all of us on the Interview Committee with your desire to do detailed Reference Checks.

Most likely, all of us combined could not match your intuition on these matters, best regards, (Client name withheld)."

I did not have to call Kent again - I knew that my Client was covered. He could no longer withhold references from me - if he wanted the job, he had to let me have them. No references - no job! Simple as that!

A few days past, and then I got them. I proceeded to call his references, and I have never ever spoken to people who were so stifled and suppressed. It seemed that they were terrified to say anything bad about him.

I also noted that his references were mostly woman who at one time or another reported to him - which means that they were primarily Subordinates, under his control.

However, there was one male who, in strong contrast to the others, was absolutely effusive about Kent's virtues. I probed as to how they met - it turned out that he was Kent's neighbor!

I asked for more references, and I wanted Superiors! Kent was becoming more agitated with me; he told me they were overseas, and he did not have their phone numbers. I suggested he get their contact information and told him phoning overseas was absolutely no problem for me - I did it *all* the time!

All in all, I ran 14 references on him - it was my turn to push back, and I was going to keep digging until I got what I wanted. Well, guess what? The 14th reference was the charm!

He was a former boss of Kent's who gave me a very honest and unguarded reference which completely contradicted the outlandish claims that Kent had made on his Resume and in his initial interview with me.

I relayed this feedback to my Client the next day - We could not move forward with his appointment. The discrepancies and oversight on Kent's part were glaring, and in time the Company hoped to go public; it would have been a problem that they simply could not have lived with.

It was back to the drawing board for me - to redo the search, but I could not have been happier, and the Candidate that I did find is still successfully working with my Client!

The moral of the story is - don't lie! No matter how tempting it is to embellish your Resume or overstate your accomplishments - don't do it! There will always be somebody (I'm not saying who…) that will go the extra mile and check the facts.

Action Steps

1. List of References

   - What kind of references do you have? Remember the four different types of References

   - How many references do you have? Ideally have four to six, mostly Superiors

   - Keep your references informed of the process - e.g. which companies you are seeing and who you are working with.

2. References should be contacted beforehand, to request their permission, and notified that they may expect calls from the people you told them about.

   Remember to give your references updated copies of your Resume and Cover Letter and never forget to thank them beforehand, for agreeing to be a reference contact for you, and afterwards for giving the reference.

3. List of Information required for Pre-Employment Checks

   - Photo ID

   - Social Insurance Number (SIN) for Canada and Social Security Number (SSN) for the USA

   - Any other information requested by the Search Consultant or Human Resources contact at the Company

CHAPTER 10

Deciding Whether To Take The Job Or Not

"Choose a job you love, and you will never have to work a day in your life."

Confucius

The Most Important Criteria To Consider Before Taking Any Job Offer

1. Corporate Culture

2. The Position

3. Salary Package

Remember this order should never change, and if you decide that salary is your highest priority; be prepared to pay the price later on...

I was recently speaking to a CEO Candidate of mine who had, a few months prior, gone through a process that I wouldn't wish on anyone. I wanted to speak to him about the experience, and ask him what he had learned so that I could pass on some tips and insights that would help others.

James is a terrific guy. Having reference checked him personally; I knew what past superiors had said about him. All my Candidates should be fortunate enough to earn such high praise from their former bosses. He was very good at what he did, and his work ethic was exemplary. In addition to that, he could work with anyone. He was excellent at building teams and getting them to work together, and his project management skills were exceptional.

However, as happens to most people, the industry that he was in experienced a downturn and work at the executive level became scarce - so when he did meet a Senior Executive who was looking for someone of James's caliber and skill set, James was delighted. He was offered a position initially as an Independent Contractor to start up a new project and take it from inception to completion - exactly the kind of work that James excelled at!

His new boss even offered him a "draft Engagement Letter" in good faith that a real offer was indeed going to be forthcoming.

This all happened while he was away on a trip attending a conference overseas. When he got back, James called me to tell me the good news, and I was very happy for him since he had been without work for almost a year, and there were no other opportunities in the pipeline.

He further mentioned that his new immediate superior, the Chairman and founder of the Company, was really looking for a CEO and had, since the "draft" Engagement Letter, spoken to James about him being the Candidate of choice for that role.

James was really pleased since it meant that he would once more be fully engaged and at the CEO level. He was told that a new Engagement Letter would be sent to him imminently. The Engagement Letter was emailed to him as promised, but the terms were no longer the same.

The salary was substantially lower and certain benefits which are customary for that level were not being given to him at all - but there was more. There was no Indemnity Clause; this meant that if anything went wrong in the Company during the time that James held the position as CEO, then he would be liable in his personal capacity for any damages that may ensue.

James said that it was normal business practice to have a proper Indemnity Clause for all businesses in this industry; it was unheard of that any member of staff, irrespective of their level, would be personally responsible for damages caused. James asked them if he could see their existing Insurance Policy because it was simply incredulous to believe that such practices were the norm. The Chairman refused to show James the Company's Insurance Policy.

James spoke to me throughout the time of negotiation with this Company. I also advised him to retain a Lawyer, which he had already done.

He said that whenever he tried to talk to the Chairman about the lack of the Indemnity Clause (which was the biggest hurdle to him signing off on a position that he really wanted) as well as other compensation related issues (also common practice in the industry) - the Chairman had no time to hear it - it was simply an annoyance to him, and James was told that he was "being difficult."

This back and forth went on for about a month - some changes were made to his Engagement Letter, but they were merely cosmetic and never addressed the truly big issues that would have exposed James to unreasonable risk.

Eventually after speaking to me, his wife, and his Lawyer, James came to the inevitable conclusion that this position, much as he wanted it, was simply not worth the aggravation of trying to argue with a boss who had only his own interests at heart and could not be bothered with even listening to his most important employee!

This experience was not without frustration and came at a considerable cost to James. He did work for this Company for about a month; he even went on business trips and was introduced as the new CEO, always on the promise that "we can work this out later on" - but nothing was ever done to completely satisfy and address James's concerns.

Eventually when things became untenable and there was no evidence that anything was going to change, James told the Chairman that he could no longer go on without the protection of a proper, legally compliant Engagement Letter and the reassurances that he needed. It never came - so James did the only sensible thing to do, he walked away from the position.

When interviewing him for this story, I assumed that James had at least been paid for the work that he did for the month that he worked for the company - he had not!

In addition to that, there were the Attorney's fees that he had incurred, not to mention the time that he had lost and the sleepless nights that he had endured.

So, I asked James the following questions:

- What was so attractive about the position in the first place?
- What did he know about the Corporate Culture?
- What did he know about the Chairman?
- What research did he do on the Company and the Chairman?
- What lessons did he learn from this experience?
- What was his take away from this?
- What advice would he give to someone, who might find themselves in a similar position?

James told me that he was immediately drawn to this opportunity since it was exactly what he was looking for…A new Project that he could build, lead, and be in charge of.

He knew little about the Corporate Culture; all his research revealed were the past successes of Principles in other Ventures that the Chairman had been involved and worked with. He found out that the Chairman had been a Banker (which is not completely uncommon in this particular industry) - other than that, James knew nothing about who the Chairman actually was and what he was like. He knew of no-one who had ever worked with him before.

The biggest lesson that he learned from this was, "Don't shake hands on a draft letter. It's better to wait." James reminded me that he had been without work for almost a year, and he was not in a position of strength. That's why he was more vulnerable and susceptible than he would normally have been to the wiles of people seeking to take advantage.

His best advice, "Don't rush in - it's better to wait, even if it means that you have to stay without work for longer!"

I'm sure you are all wondering what James is doing now. Shortly thereafter, he got a call from a small Independent Consulting Firm in the industry that was looking to increase their presence in the geographical area where James lives.

They are an honest group of people, kind, trustworthy, and fair. James is very happy working for them. He earns a decent salary for the work that he does, and is very grateful to be employed with a Company that values and respects the work that he does and the contribution that he makes on a daily basis.

The best part, when he's not travelling for work - he gets to work from home ... and be with his family. No more aggravation and no more sleepless nights!

Trust Your Feelings And Observations

Remember in Chapter 1 when "Dinosaurus Interruptus" kiboshed my interview?

Imagine if he had not shown up and the Firm did in fact make me an offer (my interview was going really well, until he walked in), and assume that I had accepted.

What if I had ended up working for *him* on most of my audits? It would have been an awful situation, and I would've been miserable! Sometimes not getting a job is a blessing in disguise...

**"Yes, we hire people with disabilities. We have a VP
who's blind to his own flaws, we have an office manager
who can't walk and chew gum at the same time, we
have an admin assistant who's deaf to criticism..."**

I Did It For Smiley!

Around the time that I met "Dinosaurus Interruptus" - I was
interviewing with a number of Audit firms to find work as an
Articled Clerk. One such Company was a medium sized firm in
Cape Town.

I had an 8:30 a.m. meeting set up to interview with a Partner at the
firm. Arriving a good 15-20 minutes before time, I walked into a
completely empty Reception area. It was a little creepy, and I felt
as if I had intruded into a place where I was not invited and
certainly not expected.

8:30 a.m. came and went, and I was now concerned that I had been
completely forgotten about, when from the back of the Reception
area, appeared an apparition with dirty, stringy blonde hair,
unkempt and uncombed, deep, black circles under her eyes
(remnants of smudged mascara from a previous time), bulbous
thighs that were threatening to split an all-too short mini-skirt, and
a skin-tight top that barely covered her essentials. She looked as if
she had arrived for work straight from a night club.

I was mortified to see someone like this in an Audit firm. What about one's front line being the Ambassador for the Company? This was incredible!

She walked back and forth to collect her thoughts and set up her day for success, yawning loudly and unbecomingly every few minutes - work was really a drag.

Next, she fetched a much needed, big mug of coffee from the kitchen, and then continued rearranging her desk, without ever looking up to acknowledge my existence!

I was the only person in the reception area - how does one miss another person sitting on a sofa directly in front of you?

Eventually, I opened my mouth and spoke up. By now it was almost 9 a.m. and I was a full 30 minutes late!

"I am here to see (and I mentioned the Partner's name)" - she turned to me as if seeing me for the first time, and I got a look that said; "Drop dead!"

Without saying a word to me, she walked down the passage to announce my arrival.

Soon the Partner came to reception to fetch me. He shook hands and was nice and friendly. "We're going to have the interview in my office," he said, "First door on your right." - I walked in, and there was another Partner (not so nice and friendly) in the office waiting for us.

For the purposes of this story, I will call one Partner "Smiley" and the other "Grouchy." Smiley invited me to sit down and immediately made me welcome.

Grouchy started interviewing with the usual kinds of questions, but he seemed pre-occupied. Smiley, on the other hand, seemed to be fully engaged and enjoying the interview - which suddenly, for no explicable reason, seemed to take a turn for the worse when Grouchy asked me why I was interested in the profession.

I tried to explain that it was a natural choice following on from my business degree. I never intended staying in the profession, but I also knew that to get my professional designation, I had to complete articles.

I did *not* mention to Grouchy that I had no intention of staying in the profession, but he must have sensed something - because all of a sudden he threw a real clanger at me that I was truly unprepared for, "Do you think you're better than our Receptionist?" he asked.

Of course, *I* was better than his Receptionist! *Everyone* I knew was better than his Receptionist - ALL my friends were better than his Receptionist - but I would never say that! However, nothing stopped me from thinking it…

He asked again, this time more pointedly. I tried to explain as best as I could that we all have different talents and want different things in life, and that everyone should do whatever makes them happy.

Grouchy was not having it - it was time to look to my left where Smiley was sitting opposite me. He was really enjoying this conversation and looked highly amused.

I took this as positive reinforcement and continued talking. Smiley even shifted in his chair and moved in closer to better hear what this fresh-faced, little "oracle of wisdom" was going to say.

"Would *you* work here as the Receptionist?" Grouchy was like a bulldog with a bone - he was not done with me or this question. "I am *not* here to interview for a Receptionist position," I countered, "I'm here to become articled!"

"So, you *do* think you're better than our Receptionist - don't you?" barked Grouchy.

Ok - so he was pushing me into a corner and he wanted an answer. I decided to give him the answer he seemed so desperately to want!

"I never ever said that I was better than anyone - but if I were the Receptionist here, I would come to work and be a million times more presentable and professional than what I saw this morning!"

I delivered that with aplomb and there it was; I had spewed it out after so carefully trying to evade answering him.

Smiley's grin was now so broad it had reached "ear-to-ear" status, and I could easily make out his dental work on the upper left hand-side. I was talking his language, and I could see that he was delighted with my response. Grouchy, on the other hand, looked as if he could slap my head off my shoulders.

I sensed something Smiley obviously knew - Grouchy was very protective of the Receptionist because they were probably related, and I was saying what Smiley wished he could have said to Grouchy, but would never have dared...

After my response, Grouchy lost interest in the interview and Smiley took over; he asked me some relevant questions and then wrapped up the interview.

Did I get the job? Of course not! My interview had turned into a comedy of faux pas as I swapped one gaffe for another. But, please cut me a little slack here; I had no guidelines for interviewing and was still using my training wheels...

I had clearly crossed a line by disparaging their Receptionist. Was I upset? Not really because I realized that I would not be happy working for that Firm. I based this on two very specific things:

1. How I felt, and
2. What I had observed.

I knew that I would never have become friends with the Receptionist, although we were probably contemporaries. There would have been no love for me coming from the Panda-eyed, thunder-thighed, dancing queen, especially after Grouchy had shared my unvarnished opinion with her.

In addition to that, I saw from the first few seconds of the three of us being together in Smiley's office, that the Partners were not in sync about anything. The one contradicted the other and vice versa - they were continually bickering and arguing with one another, and they were doing this in front of me.

I would never have been happy in a Corporate Culture of discourtesy and dissent.

Why is Corporate Culture so Important?

Corporate Culture is the "essence" of a Company. The shared values of its Members: their goals, visions, ideals, and business practices. Most of all, it is characterized by the way the Members of that Company treat each other.

The Corporate Culture is governed by a set of beliefs that are crafted, developed, and designed by Senior Management. In other instances, the whole organization gets to vote on what they believe 'the Company's Core Values should be." The basic premise of all Core Values is the ideal to which companies aspire, in terms of how their people relate to one another, how they engage and interact with each other, as well as their outside Clients and Stakeholders. In other words, how do the Employees treat people inside and outside the Company?

Knowing how you will be treated if you work for a certain Company *before* you accept a position is critically important.

But how do you find that out?

By doing all of the following:

1. Know What You Want

Knowing what you want in terms of your next position is absolutely essential. If you don't take the trouble to find out what environment suits you best - you'll never flourish in a job. You simply have to know, and you find this out when you make yourself your most important project!

If you don't know exactly what you want to do or you're too "laissez faire" to really care, be prepared to spend your life doing other people's agenda.

You don't want to be tossed around in the job market, like flotsam and jetsam, trying to find a place where you can just do your work in peace.

You have to be more self-directed than that. The most successful people always know exactly what they want to do and what they absolutely would not even consider doing.

2. Research

Find out everything you can about the Company, its Senior Executive team, their respective backgrounds, reviews on them, and as much as you can from people who have worked with them.

This seems like an awful lot of work to do, but doing this will save you time, money, and heartache in the long term. It is so worth it to make this an absolute priority in your job search.

If you are working with a Headhunter, they will give you some information on what they know about their Client, but *you* still need to do your own research. There is never a substitute for doing your own due diligence.

There are websites like http://www.glassdoor.com that I strongly recommend because you can look up a Company and see what they have on their website, what current employees and past employees are saying about them.

3. Audit The Integrity Of Senior Management

When I was at University, we had the Dean of the Commerce Faculty come and speak to us about integrity. He spent the entire lecture talking about how critically important the concept of integrity was and how we should never compromise our integrity - because once we have lost it, we could never get it back!

To further drive the point home, he created a hypothetical example. "One day," he said, "You will have left the profession, and many of you will be starting your own companies; you will be so thrilled to have a new Client and will want to take on as many Clients as you can handle - Don't!" he admonished. "Don't take on a Client until you have audited the integrity of the Senior Management Team!"

I never forgot that lecture, or that lesson, and it stood me in very good stead when I started my Executive Search Firm and was taking on new Clients - I do NOT take on every Client, just because of that lecture. It was one of the best lessons I ever learnt!

If you get the slightest inkling that a Senior Executive who interviewed you is *not* completely honest - walk away right now! This is not the time to give someone the benefit of the doubt because you need the job!

4. Social Networking Sites

Look at the Company's social networking sites, like LinkedIn, Facebook and Twitter - this will give you an impression of their branding - are they innovative, creative and leading edge or are they more staid and formal?

See if you know anyone who works there, and even if you don't, try and reach out to people via LinkedIn. Let them know that you are interested in working for the Company.

Ask if they wouldn't mind speaking to you privately. You will be surprised how helpful people are - usually at opposite sides of the spectrum.

Those that love the Company and those that hate the Company are more likely to be willing to speak to you. The first group out of pride (and perhaps employee incentives if their Company is hiring!) and the latter group, because they don't want to see someone else get burnt.

5. Ask at the Interview

At the end of an interview, the Interviewer or Panel will always ask the Candidate if they have any questions. Ask about the Corporate Culture. Ask the Interviewer why they accepted a position with this Company, what they love most about working for the Company, and what they wished the Company would do differently.

Ask salient questions. I was doing a search several years ago for a dynamic Company in the financial services industry. At lunch time, the committee and I sat around the table talking, and I was curious as to why some of the VPs had joined the Company. I asked one of them, and he gave me a flippant answer - "Because the coffee is good here," he said facetiously.

Now, he wasn't interviewing for a position; he already worked there - but his answer was annoying; I learned nothing. I mention this because I want to illustrate how *not* to squander an opportunity to ask the right questions!

Ask about the characteristics of the top performers, what kinds of people do well, and of course, what types of people would not do well in this environment. You want to find out where you'd fit in. If you're a "steady Eddie" - you are not going to fit into a fast paced environment. It will seem rushed and overwhelming. The objective is for you to find a position in an environment that is perfect for you.

Ask if you may meet employees that are currently working for the Company. If the Company is proud of their culture, it won't be a problem. In fact, they will be glad to introduce you to some of their employees because you will be meeting additional people who could be ambassadors for the Company and reinforce why *that* particular Company is a great place to work.

If they are not in favor of you meeting with anyone - be on your guard; there must be something they wish to keep well hidden from future prospects.

6. Non-Scientific Guidance

We all have a built-in guidance system; intuition that tells us when things just don't seem right! Trust your feelings...

I tell my coaching Clients to be particularly vigilant to everything that goes on when they present themselves for an interview. Look at the offices, observe people walking through the reception area. Do they look happy, do people smile at each other, make small talk, and greet one another?

Do not have your head buried in a magazine or the newspaper. You are losing an opportunity to evaluate your environment. Listen to how the Receptionist answers the phone - is she happy, engaging and polite to callers? Does she interact nicely with the people who walk up to her desk and talk to her?

Why is this important? It may seem trivial. Let's just say that the Receptionist does not determine the Corporate Culture - No, she did not decide how it should be, but she was hired to match what the Company was all about. She is their ambassador, their front line, their branding, and image specialist!

Your experience with the Company's first line of defense may well be a sign of how you will be treated, should you accept a position there.

When I ask Candidates to think and tell me every little detail about their interview experience,

I cannot tell you how many Candidates will tell me, after *not* getting a position, that not even the Receptionist was nice to them.

Your next reference point should be with your Interviewer or Interview Panel, or in some cases where you are interviewed by several people individually, ask each what they love about the Company and why they joined. Their answers can be illuminating.

When you are being interviewed, see how the Panel members talk to each other and whether they generally agree or vehemently disagree. There is nothing wrong with people having opposing viewpoints, but it's how they sort them out and come to mutual agreement in deciding what is best for the Company that matters.

I have been on some really interesting Search Committees where the Members of the Panel had conflicting ideas about which person should be the winning Candidate. The bickering and fighting that goes on behind the scenes makes me frightened for the Candidate that will end up working there. The debriefing sessions in particular can get very spirited!

For a Candidate, the interview itself is a time to carefully observe how people interact. It will give you a good sense of whether the Corporate Culture is one of coherence and collaboration or discord and dissent.

Why Corporate Culture Is Given the Highest Priority

When you work in a corporate environment, you could easily end up spending more than 50-60 hours a week with the people that you work with, so it's essential that you trust, respect, and admire them. It's also important that they feel the same way about you.

The feeling has to be absolutely mutual, and when it is - you have synergy like you've never seen before. The employees thrive and are proud to be a part of the Company. They champion the benefits of working for that organization and everyone wins!

Sadly, the converse is equally true. When things are bad, they are toxic. Working in such an environment can slowly kill you.

The Position

You know it's imperative that you do work that you love because that's one thing that will guarantee your success. However, even if you've found the job of your dreams, there is one thing that can thwart your ascendancy - the Corporate Culture in which you work!

So, even if the position is wonderful and you honestly love the work that you do - you will not be working alone and will inevitably need the collaboration or buy-in for your ideas and projects to flourish. If every time you need that, you are either stonewalled or meet with opposition - you will not last.

The fact that you delight in the work that you do will not be enough to succeed in an environment that is not supportive.

Salary Package

Everyone wants to be valued for the work that they do, and their value in a Corporate Environment is inevitably measured by what they earn.

We would all love a salary package that is exceedingly generous and benefits like the Tech Companies offer in Silicon Valley, but in the absence of that, you at least want a salary that is competitive with regards to similar companies in your industry.

When you are not paid a market related salary, you will always be open to other opportunities and calls from Headhunters - because you are not paid what you're worth. When you're underpaid, you start to feel underappreciated and resentful.

No matter how wonderful the Executive of the Company is, how fabulous it is to work there, or even how rewarding the work is - sooner or later, you will take a call from someone who will lure you away, and you would be absolutely right to do so!

Action Steps

1. Go back to your original list of what you wanted and expected from your next prospective employer. Decide whether this offer meets your criteria in terms of your new evaluation system. Use it as a filter for all your job opportunities.

   - Corporate Culture
   - The Position
   - Salary Package

2. Remember, this priority should never change.

3. If the offer does not meet your expectation or you feel this organization is not a good fit culturally, or the position itself is limiting in terms of future career advancement - walk away!

Don't be scared to walk away; no-one ever feels happy when they are expected to accept unreasonable compromises.

There are certain things that you should never compromise: your integrity, standards, and values because you will lose them and the price of losing what is irreplaceable is simply too high. No job is worth that!

"Dan, you are my most valuable employee.
Your ineptitude consistently raises the
self-esteem of everyone you work with."

CHAPTER 11

Negotiating Compensation Package

"Strive not to be a success, but rather to be of value."

Albert Einstein

Salary negotiation is one of the most feared and stressful parts of the interview for Candidates, but it need not be, provided you are well prepared.

If you have been referred through a third party, such as a Headhunter, the Client will already have been informed as to what you are currently earning and what you are looking for. The third party will be doing a fair amount of the negotiation on your behalf.

That being said, you should still expect to negotiate. Like everything else, it will always come down to the research, due diligence, and preparation that *you*, as the Candidate, have done.

If you have approached a Company directly, then you have an even greater need to ensure that you have thoroughly prepared to negotiate the best compensation that you can for yourself.

Remember, no-one will ever be more emotionally or financially invested in your success than you!

What You Should Do

1. Know Exactly What You Currently Earn

This seems so self-explanatory, but I cannot tell you how many times I have interviewed a Candidate, and when we get to this part of the interview, they know what their base salary is, but are completely ignorant as to the details of the rest of their package.

If you are currently employed, you must know exactly what the value of your benefits are. You see, to *get* what you want - you have to *know* what your starting point is.

You do this by analyzing down to the most minute detail what you're *currently* worth in terms of the benefits that you get now!

If you are in transition, you must know what the *total value* of your last salary package was.

To sum this up succinctly:

1. Know exactly what you current salary is (base and benefits)

2. Know what your worth is on the open market - comparable to similar positions in your niche

3. Know what you want

You cannot possibly negotiate up if you have no starting point. I am not encouraging you to be petty, but just to be prepared. Break down your compensation package into base salary and benefits. As best as you can, value those benefits individually.

I once had a Candidate who was made a generous offer that he immediately wanted to accept, but I asked him to think about it and sleep on the offer. When he had time the next day to carefully go over the offer - he realized that although the base salary was considerably more than he was currently making, the medical benefits were not nearly as good as his current Employer offered.

He had a "special needs" child, and the medical benefits became a deal breaker - he simply could not accept the new offer as the differential in base salary was still not enough to cover the additional costs that he would have to pay, for his son's medical needs.

2.   Know How Much You're Worth

Your due diligence should include research on sites such as Payscale.com, Glassdoor.com and Indeed.com

Make a list of comparable companies that match the same criteria of your current employer and your position in terms of:

- Industry
- Company size
- Position title
- Education and professional designations
- Skills sets
- Number of years of experience
- How many people you supervise

In addition, make considerations for whether the industry you are working in is booming and talent is in short supply, or conversely if it is in recession and the market is flooded with people looking for work.

3.   Know What You Want

Once you know exactly what the *value* of your current package is, *and* you know what you are *worth* in the job market - then it is easy to decide what you *want*.

You should have a minimum in terms of the lowest acceptable salary level and benefits that you would consider. Anything below this "minimum acceptable salary" would be the point at which you would walk away if the Client could not match this salary level.

I'm not suggesting you should take this at all, but it represents a "floor" below which it does not make sense for you to leave a current employer or take the position, even if you are in transition. You should always weigh up the opportunity cost of taking one particular position against waiting a little longer for a better offer to present itself in the future.

Remember James's story and his advice, "It is better to wait, even if you don't have work immediately!"

Of course, there is no hard and fast rule for what one should *always* do. It will always depend on the personal circumstances of the Candidate and the upside potential of the opportunity being considered.

Then have an "ideal salary package" that represents the remuneration you would be very happy to receive.

Most Candidates and Clients find a compromise somewhere between the two, but knowing the above information is essential to bolstering your ability to negotiate and "counteroffer" if, and when, the time comes.

Also take into account that no two companies ever provide exactly the same benefits; that's why you also need to know the value of your benefits (as part of your total earnings package) and know *which* benefits are most important to you.

You will inevitably need to compromise on some benefits to get additional advantages elsewhere, either in increased base salary or different benefits.

Being prepared and knowing what you want will put you in very good stead to ensure that the final salary package that you accept is at least equitable to what you really want and hopefully substantially better than what you expected!

What to do when a Company is interested in you and a job offer is forthcoming

When a Company has indicated that they would like to make you an offer, allow them to broach the subject of salary first. They will probably ask you what you are currently earning or if you are in transition, what you earned at your last position - then they will want to know what you are looking for; that's why you *have* to know the value of your current or previous salary package as well as your worth compared to industry norms.

When asked what you are looking for, give them the top end of the range of what you are looking for and wait to see their reaction.

You can always negotiate down - but it's really hard, negotiating up!

If they balk at the amount and tell you that it would be a stretch for them, let the Company know that you have done your research, and that's what you are worth in the marketplace based on what similar companies in your industry are paying for your type of position, skill set, and experience.

Mention your past successes in areas that you know are very important to them, and reassure them that you have much to offer and would love to be able to help their Company in the same way. Let them know that you are able to address their most urgent needs and that you can contribute immediately!

Most companies are impressed when Candidates are prepared and have a good sense of their worth - it's a sign that you are an achiever and that you are in control of your career.

Always let them know that you are really pleased that they have extended an offer and that you would very much like to work for the Company. You should always be grateful, whether you end up accepting the offer or not. Your level of professionalism is paramount to maintaining your reputation.

If the Company comes back, and they are adamant that your amount is simply outside of their range, ask them what they had in mind as far as an offer is concerned. Let them know that you are flexible and that many factors will go into your decision before accepting an offer.

Stress that the Corporate Culture has to be a good fit, the kind of environment where you would thrive in, and the work itself has to be interesting and exceptionally rewarding.

You don't want the Company representative to think that you are only concerned about the money - so emphasize that the money in itself is certainly not your highest priority.

However, it still remains a measure of your worth, and for you to be able to offer your best to a prospective employer, all three factors have to work for you: the corporate culture, the position, and the compensation that you will be paid.

Let them know how much you loved meeting the people who interviewed you and that you can see yourself really fitting in well with the group.

Mention that even though there is a differential between what they had in mind to offer you and what you are looking for, you'd still appreciate receiving an offer; be excited and let them know that you are looking forward to receiving their offer.

Wait Before You Counter

Once you've received their letter of engagement, take your time to reflect and carefully analyze every aspect of your offer.

Look beyond the base salary and see whether the benefits (sign-up bonus, stock options, paid vacation, 401 K Plan, and other benefits) add up to what you feel is acceptable.

If not, then you have a point and reason for a counteroffer. Even if you are disappointed, stay cool, calm, and collected - this is not a sign of weakness, but of professionalism.

You do not want to be the Candidate that the Company remembers for "exploding on them" because you were disappointed with their offer to you. You will look childish and immature, and they will immediately regret that they made you an offer in the first place.

Before you think of discussing your counteroffer, build your "business case" to justify it, then talk to them and do the following:

Thank the Company for their offer, but let them know that you really believe you are worth more, and then mention the amount that you had in mind.

Give them reasons for believing you are worth more.

- List your specific achievements and past successes in an area of expertise that is critical for them. Only do this if you *are* an authority expert in that field.

- Let them know that what you've done for your previous Company - you can do for them also.

- Tell them that you are ideally suited to the position and that you will work diligently to exceed their expectations. What you'd like in return from them is to realize that in order for you to feel appreciated and valued, you'd like a salary package that is commensurate with what you've done in the past and what they can expect from you in the future.

Then wait to see what they come back with. Either the package will increase or they won't budge.

If they don't increase your package, ask whether there is any room for increased benefits, additional paid vacation, a bigger sign up bonus, etc. You are looking to see if there is any compromise and willingness on their side to accommodate you and be flexible.

Should the Company not budge at all on their original offer, and the salary is far lower than you had expected, then it's time to "read the writing on the wall" - either the Company:

1. Simply does not have the budget for someone at your level; in which case, they were leading you on because this information ought to have been known long before you got to this stage, or

2. The Company is completely inflexible. See this as a sign of things to come. You do not want to work for a Company that is rigid, unaccommodating, and unyielding - you will never be able to shine and rise to your greatest heights in this kind of environment.

It's time to walk away and refocus your efforts on opportunities that secure results and are much more rewarding!

What A Company Will Do When They *Really* Want A Candidate

I can tell you first hand, a Company that wants a Candidate will move Heaven and Earth - if the perceived value is in that Candidate, and the Company really wants them. Of course, they have to have the budget as well.

One of my last searches prior to emigrating from South Africa was a CFO search. I was working directly with the CEO who had known me for a number of years. He wanted to pay the equivalent salary of $150,000 which was market related at the time - this was 20 years ago.

I interviewed several Candidates within that range, and then saw one exceptional Candidate that was earning $250,000 - well outside the range that he initially wanted to pay.

Since we had known each other for a while, I knew the CEO's temperament; he was dynamic, but equally demanding, with a low tolerance for someone that did not get the job done!

When I went to present Candidates, I had three excellent Candidates in the $150,000 range and he was very keen on them, but then he noticed that I had one more file that I had not presented to him.

"What do you have in your hand there?" he asked.

"Colin, I know you will be happy with any of the Candidates that I have given you; they are all good - but the one I'm holding in my hand is absolutely exceptional! The only problem is that she is earning over $100,000 more than you are prepared to pay."

"You're kidding!" he said, "I thought $150,000 was a really good salary."

"It is - for a good Candidate, but superstars cost more!"

"Let me see that!" he said, snatching the file out of my hand. For the next few minutes, his eyebrows did the talking while he carefully perused her Resume… "She earns $250,000 dollars?" he asked, incredulously.

"Yes," I said, "And she's a flaming red head - so don't mess with her!"

Colin laughed, "Okay - set me up with them" - he mused. "I can do Tuesday next week - this is an important position, so let me block out the whole day and let's do this!" he said with typical fortitude.

Now, I obviously don't do this with every Client, but I knew Colin's nature and his temperament. I knew the bossy little red-head would be an equal match for him; furthermore, he was the kind of man that both respected women and also really did not care *who* got the job as long as it was absolutely the best person for the role!

Someone who could keep up with him and pre-empt what was going to be important even before he had discussed it with them. The fit had to be right for the Corporate Culture that Colin created, and the person had to be up to the position and his demands.

Guess who got the job? You're right! The "bossy little red-head," and she would not come down one iota in salary to take it - Yup, Colin, my "alpha male" Client came up more than $100,000 to get her, and it was a great match!

What You Should Never Do

1.   Don't Embellish Your Earnings and Lie!

You already know how I feel about this...

We live in an age where it is incredibly easy to find out the truth. If you are found to have lied after you've started working for the Company - expect to miss out on future promotions (if the Company still wants to keep you) - it could even cost you your job!

Employers have a very low tolerance for liars, and with the job market as competitive as it is, there may be a dozen or more Candidates willing to take your place, should you be asked to leave.

2.   Don't Discuss Salary at an Interview!

I will qualify exactly what I mean by this. Obviously, if you are asked what you are looking for in terms of your salary expectations - answer truthfully. Always be honest. I just want you to think strategically and let logic prevail here...

I don't want *you* to be the one that brings up salary first!

Initiating the salary discussion is like asking someone to marry you when you don't even know if they like you yet!

Wait until you have feedback that the Company wants to make you an offer.

This is easier if you have been put forward by a Headhunter. You will receive feedback immediately after the interview to let you know whether the Company is interested in you or not.

However, if you have approached the Company directly, the best advice I can give you is: Be patient, keep busy pursuing other leads, and always remain calm and confident; never show that you are desperate.

The Company is generally never in as dire a need to hire as a Candidate is to receive a letter of offer. So, the way to mitigate the stress of waiting and worrying about whether you got the job is to have many "irons in the fire," job opportunities and leads at varying stages in the search process.

Having several options will also give you more confidence, and your quiet self-assurance, poise, and ease will not go unnoticed by the people who have met you.

3. Don't Lie About Having Another Offer!

Several years ago I was headhunting for the IT department of a very large Professional Services Firm. The Company was looking for someone with very specific skills, and I cast my net wide to find the best Candidates.

Out of the blue, I got a call from another person, not a Headhunter, but a Consultant and Founder of an IT Consulting Firm to say that he had seen my advertisement and that he had the "perfect" Candidate.

I did not know this person at all, but I wanted to keep an open mind and not exclude any Candidate that was really good. My mandate is always to find the best people in the market place for all my Clients.

This would mean that I would split my fee with him, but I was still keen to see his Candidate, so I agreed to interview him and if he was indeed "perfect," I would put him forward for an interview with my Client.

I also explained to this Consultant that the Corporate Culture at the Professional Service's Firm, especially within *their* IT department, was young and dynamic - so a fairly mature person would not be a good fit.

He said he understood perfectly and assured me that the Candidate was no more than 38 years old, which was already *very* mature in comparison to the average age of the group - but this did not put me off.

Deciding to do a telephone interview first, I called his Candidate and almost dropped the phone when he answered. He was from Eastern Europe and had a big burly voice that sounded thunderous - but after talking to him for an hour, I had grown extremely fond of Boris, who I will affectionately refer to as my "Russian bear," and decided to bring him in for a face-to-face meeting.

When he arrived, I saw immediately that he wasn't *even* 58 years old "in the shade". Now, age is not normally ever an issue, but my Client had stressed that the right person would have to fit in with the very young dynamic of the group.

In terms of *this* benchmark, Boris was an appallingly bad fit. However, he had the right experience, and I am a stickler for giving people the benefit of the doubt (way too often); besides, Boris was incredibly likeable and charming!

On the day of the final interviews, myself and a young Search Committee of "30-something year olds" got together to interview the Candidates.

When it was Boris's turn, I saw that, in all honesty, it wasn't just about his age; he was like a huge bear, with the slow gait and deliberateness of movement that corresponded to his mammalian metaphor.

He was no match for the exuberant, high energy vibe that was characteristic of the group or the other Candidates, but as I said before, he was good at his job and by putting him forward; I felt that at least he was an inch closer to finding the right opportunity, but it would *not* be with this Client!

That being said, everyone was nice to Boris, and he obviously had no inkling that he was unsuited to the group. As I was walking him to the elevator after the interview, Boris turned to me in his characteristic burly voice and said, "Let them know that I have other offers!" "You should tell them that there is another Company that is making me an offer now!"

I reassured Boris that I would, and was secretly pleased that he had other opportunities, but there was something that was off, that at the time, I could simply *not* put my finger on…then he added further that the offers were "*verrrry* good" in his heavy Russian accent. I nodded acceptingly, "I will tell them".

When the interviews were finished, it was time for the debriefing session with the Interview Committee. No one said a bad word about Boris other than to concur with each other that he was simply "not the right fit" for this department or the Firm as a whole.

The next day, I got back to the IT Consultant who had put him forward and wanted to give him some constructive feedback. "Firstly," I said, "You deceived me by lying about Boris's age; he isn't 38 and will never see 38 again. He laughed guiltily and protested, "But he's good at what he does!"

"That's not the point - everyone that interviewed yesterday is exceptionally good at what they do, and they are also a good fit for the Corporate Culture of the Firm and that specific department! I had made this clear when you wanted me to present your Candidate, but you lied to me and put him forward anyway!

Fortunately, Boris tells me he has other offers in the pipeline - *very* good offers!"

The line suddenly went really quiet. "What offers did he tell you about?" he asked suspiciously.

"He did not tell me *anything* about the offers, just that he had several offers, and that he was being made a *very* good offer even as we spoke."

It had suddenly gone deathly quiet; all I heard was the IT Consultant breathing heavily as he processed this newly received information. Judging from the wall of silence, I realized that the con had just been conned!

Boris had no other offers, he just told a lie to create the impression that he was in high demand. He was going to use the notion that he was being made a "*very* good" offer to get me to push my Client into making a quick decision to hire him - now this may have worked, except that my Client never wanted him in the first place!

A few days later, Boris called me on the pretext that he was waiting for feedback. I told him that I had delivered the feedback to the IT Consultant right after the interview.

But, as Boris was already on the phone and rejection is never easy, I told him that he was a good Candidate, but they saw many very good Candidates, and selected one that the Search Committee felt was a better fit for their department.

He immediately asked me if I had any other opportunities for him. "What happened to your *very* good offer?" I asked, without skipping a beat.

He was very coy about it, and I pushed right back and reminded him about our conversation at the elevator - "What about ALL the other offers you were telling me about?" I demanded. "I mean one can fall through - but ALL of them?"

Boris was clearly caught out in a blatant lie, but at no point did my Russian bear from the cold war give up the truth...Perhaps he was

better suited to the KGB than an IT position with one of my
Clients!

4.   Don't Refuse to Share What You Are Currently Earning!

Share what your current salary information is with your
Headhunter at the interview when asked. It is impossible to go out
and bat for a Candidate and try to negotiate a higher salary, when
you won't tell us what you earn!

Don't play games by withholding this information; its frustrating
dealing with someone who won't be completely honest.
Furthermore, the Clients expect that we know this information
about our Candidates. It makes it much easier to make informed
decisions when this information is available and transparent to
everyone.

Evelyn was a CFO Candidate that was referred to me by a CEO
who was working with me during his job search.

She had a really good Resume, and I was keen to meet her. Evelyn
came in for an interview and we clicked right away. I really
enjoyed interviewing her, and I felt that she appreciated the detail
that I went into and the time that I took to get to know her better.

We discussed extensively the kind of industries and positions that
she was open to. Spending time with her was very pleasant until I
asked her what her last salary was…It was as if I had crossed a
line, from whence there was no retreat - the walls went up, and she
was NOT going to answer that question!

I probed as to why she was so hell bent on *not* revealing what she
earned, and her explanation surprised me.

Whenever she had interviewed in the past and was asked for her
salary information, the prospective employer never offered her
what she *wanted*; instead, they offered her a small increase based
on what she *currently earned*.

Evelyn was so affronted by these insulting offers that she had
come to the conclusion that she was better off not working
permanently, but rather doing temporary work.

If she preferred to have the freedom of doing temporary assignments, there was nothing wrong with that, and I supported whatever suited her best. The problem was that she really wasn't happy doing temporary assignments since the work was sporadic and did not afford her the financial security that she wanted. So, what was a girl to do?

Evelyn decided that she was *not,* under *any* circumstances, going to tell anyone what she earned; rather, she would simply state what she *wanted* in terms of earnings, and then they would *have* to pay her what she wanted!

No future employer would be sidetracked by what she was earning - "No!" Evelyn was done with that, and the way she would control the situation was to emphatically refuse to tell anyone what she earned. That way, no one could pay her less than she wanted.

And her price tag? - $250,000 per annum and nothing less!

As you can imagine, no future employer *has* to pay you what you want. Although Evelyn was finding that out, she was still not prepared to budge or reconsider her strategy!

A prospective employer will pay you based on:

1. What you *currently earn* (which, most of the time, is a yard stick for what you are worth)

2. What you are *worth* based on what the job market is paying for your particular skill set based on the factors previously mentioned

3. What you *want*, provided they have the budget, and you can justify your salary requirements based on your unique skill set and past history of success.

I explained to Evelyn, that her logic was flawed since no employer *had* to pay her what she wanted. I also asked her how she justified the $250,000 price tag for her services.

She was a good Candidate, but she was nothing special or out of the ordinary, nor did she possess any unique skill set that was in high demand.

Evelyn never thought that she would have to justify her desired earnings of $250,000. All she had was a strategy for "punishing" people who might seek to offer her a position at seemingly less than what she wanted or felt she deserved.

I asked her what her reason was for wanting to meet me - She believed that I could represent her and *make* a prospective employer pay her what she wanted!

I tried to articulate to Evelyn that even *I* could not go out and negotiate on her behalf if we negotiated from a position of dishonesty and distrust.

I explained to her, as nicely as I could, that withholding salient information, such as salary, made *her* look untrustworthy!

After speaking to her on this one particular issue for hours on end, I still could not get her to change her mind - it was her way or the highway! The end of the story was that I simply walked away. It was just too frustrating, and I was not prepared to trade my reputation for her illogical demands.

Remember, no one has to do your bidding. As in any relationship, there has to be give and take (not only take), and the best relationships start off on a basis of honesty and trust.

Where there is no honesty, there is no basis for trust. Where there is no trust, it makes no sense to have a relationship!

5. Don't Accept a Verbal Offer, And Then Renegotiate Your Offer After the Client Accepts Your Confirmation

Randy was a really interesting Candidate. He was young, exciting, very bright, well educated, and arrogant. The kind of person that is so impressive when you meet them, but the longer you know them, the more your contempt and dislike for them grows.

He was working for a big public Company, and I head-hunted him for a Client of mine, a much smaller public Company.

Randy was interested in my Client since he thought that a smaller Company would be less bureaucratic, and he would have more opportunity to do what he wanted.

I did a very detailed interview with Randy and then personally ran his references which were very good; there was nothing underhand - he seemed absolutely above board and checked out really well. It was time to introduce him to the Senior Executive Team at my Client.

I was not on the Interview Committee as I normally am because sometimes a Client has their own preference for building a relationship or getting to know a Candidate, and I believe in always doing what is best for my Client.

When I was interviewing Randy and it got to the part where I ask about salary package - he was more than happy to tell me what he was earning. Fortunately my Client's offer was more - not considerably more, but more than he was currently earning, so I knew that he would be interested, as my Client had a lot more to offer, other than salary.

Randy let me know in no uncertain terms that he was more interested in the Company and position; money was not really his priority - he was more about the opportunity! Music to my ears!

In the interview, he was super relaxed - like a man in a position of power. He had a terrific job with a top Company, and he was interviewing for another - one might even say that he was decidedly in a position of strength. He behaved as if he was in full control, with sarcastic barbs directed at me; which I found insulting and he, amusing…

Randy was arrogant and rude. He functioned with impunity on a spectrum of obnoxiousness, from being mildly obnoxious (on the extreme left) to being thoroughly obnoxious (on the extreme right) and everything in between, on all levels of the continuum!

He was smart enough to temper and bridle his speech when he was not sure of the Company; however, after a few drinks loosened him up, and he became more familiar with the Company around him, the pendulum swung dangerously to the right.

And when he was in this state, he started saying things that others found highly offensive!

Fortunately, the "powers" that be, liked his background and spunk and made him an offer - the *full amount* of what he had asked for. The Chairman himself put his stamp of approval on the deal, and I thought that for all intents and purposes the contract was signed, sealed, and delivered. Randy had given his word, and he had accepted a tacit agreement.

I received a call the day after, his night out, from one of the Company officials in charge of being the "liaison" between me and the Senior Executive of the Company to tell me that the Company was very happy to extend an offer and please would I convey this news to Randy. I was reminded that Randy had already let everyone know that he had "accepted."

When I called Randy to let him know the good news, he said that he was *not* taking the offer - I was mortified! "But you accepted last night!"; I countered.

"Yes," he said, "but now I want you to go back and renegotiate for me - I want more money! If you know how to negotiate - this should not be too difficult for you," he added with a good dose of sarcasm.

I was livid, but I still felt that as he was my Candidate, I had to at least try and see whether there was any chance that they might consider increasing his salary somewhat. I ended up speaking to the CEO who was really angry and certainly not prepared to even entertain the idea.

He felt that Randy was already offered too much and was not enamored with Randy's performance the night before. "There is no chance that we would even consider going up," he said. "There are far more deserving people who work for the Company and earn less than he does. This is our best and final offer," he said with absolute finality.

I let Randy know. He was still in game playing mode - but eventually, he realized that there would be no more money forthcoming, and with great reluctance signed the contract.

Why You Should Never Do This

Going back on your word is never a good strategy. This is not the way to get more money or benefits out of a Company. It certainly is not a way to enhance your reputation.

You negotiate beforehand - but once you have verbally agreed to a contract - you should always keep your word. Keeping your word is a sign of your integrity. Without integrity, your word means nothing and no-one will trust you!

Besides, if you "call a Company's bluff," they may just roll the dice, knowing you have played them and withdraw their offer - and then you have lost everything!

"You've described yourself as a 'free thinker'.
That's good because we can't afford to pay you."

Additional Notes On Salary

Most of this chapter focused on negotiating one's salary when you are accepting a new position because the premise is that it is part of the Job Search process. However, what if you are already working for a Company, your performance review is coming up shortly, and you wish to be well prepared for your "Salary Review" discussion? Then you should do the following:

First Things First - *Who* Are You Really Working For?

Before I get into *"What"* you should be doing, I want to talk about *"Why"* you should be doing exactly what I will tell you to do.

Do you see a pattern in each chapter? There is a strategy for doing every single aspect of the Job Search as well as you can, in order to increase the probability of getting exactly what you want.

Having a strategy is about having a specific plan to do things right if you want to secure a successful outcome. For most people in transition, a successful outcome represents a fabulous job, with the right Company, at a salary level that affords them the lifestyle that they desire.

Now, let's start with the end result in mind - *that fabulous job!*

When you know exactly "why" you want that job, then you have a clear-cut reason for going after it and when you have a clear-cut reason, you are exponentially more motivated to do what you need to do, to get it!

But let's say that you already have the position and have been working for the Company for a while, and your performance review is coming up which is always tied to your salary review. Let's just say that you aren't as motivated as you were when you first got the job…

This begs the question. How do you negotiate a higher salary now?

Well, before I show you how to negotiate a better salary when you are already in the position - let's first discuss what happened to your "why"? Did you know that your *"why"* is directly correlated to your *motivation*?

As your *motivation* drops off, so does the reason (your *"why"*) for wanting the job in the first place. It becomes more dimmed with time…

Which leads us to the next question - why did your motivation drop off?

Let me guess, your motivation dropped off for a myriad of reasons: the position became more pressured, the Company is underfunded, your boss left and you can't stand the new one that took his place, the work is just not rewarding any more, and you are underappreciated and over worked.

None of your accomplishments get noticed, only the mistakes - for which you are disparaged and humiliated in front of your team. I could go on and on, and ALL those reasons are valid.

I really do empathize; however, what if I told you something that would change how you felt about your work, your position in the Company, and how you saw and valued yourself.

A simple statement - brilliant in its simplicity and absolute in its truth...

You Are Always Working For Yourself!

You know that one person who is with you 24/7, who knows your deepest secrets and wildest aspirations, and who still never leaves you or thinks you're crazy?

Why would you short change someone so incredibly loyal and supportive, loving and caring, motivating and understanding, someone who always has your back and would never desert you when you needed them most - whose depth of feeling for you is immeasurable, and whose love for you, incomprehensible? It's time to give *that* person a chance...because they deserve it more than anyone!

So, next time you are assigned to a project, forget that you're doing it for your boss or the Board of Directors, or whoever - the truth is you're really doing it for yourself!

Set the bar high, and then deliver beyond what you thought was possible. Set aside some time to segment the various areas in your life that you want to work on and improve. If you need to take courses in specific areas to increase your expertise - do so. You are investing in yourself!

When you look at life from this perspective, even if you are currently working in a corporate environment for a superior that does not appreciate you, it does not matter - you are always working for yourself, and whatever new skills you acquire, you get to take them with you!

Life is never static - be prepared, keep learning and growing!

How To Negotiate For An Internal Salary Review

You will feel differently about your next Salary Review now that you have your motivation back because you have discovered the best "why" in the world!

You will be negotiating from a position of strength - because now you understand that your superior or the Board of Directors does not really look at things from your perspective, only from *theirs!*

When you understand how *they* think, then you can plan accordingly. They want results, and they want to see results before they will consider giving you anything.

If you're already working for the Company - then you know what the challenges are and the most critical issues that come up and need addressing. You start planning on how to negotiate for your next salary review right after your last salary review, and then you need to forget about your upcoming salary review!

That's right! Forget about your salary review, and look at what's behind it. Look at the mandate that you've been given, the milestones that you are expected to meet, the crises that you will have to address, and the teams that you have to build - focus on that!

I say this with one caveat - keep a journal of all these accomplishments - no-one will ever be more proud of what you have achieved, than you. Because of this, they will never fully understand or know the depth of sacrifice, you made to reach these standards.

You must keep records because you will need it to build a "business case" to justify that you are worth a really decent increase in salary.

That "business case" that you build is one of the most valuable assets that you have - so guard it carefully, and keep it safely away from prying eyes. It is sacrosanct; treat it like a living document - it should grow with each accomplishment.

Now when you meet with your superior and have your performance and salary review, you are prepared; you know that you've had a great year and done exemplary work. You will walk into that meeting with a list of your departments' accomplishments, both yours personally and your teams'.

Get excited about your performance review; you are in a position of strength. When your superior asks you how you feel you've done - smile and say, "Great!" because it will be true.

Expect that your superior will leave out several of your accomplishments and harp on a few things that he or she thought you could have done better - but you will have your "list of achievements" with you, and you will have the details that your superior doesn't - because they could never be as invested in your success as you are!

You will speak to your boss about your team and the incredible year your department had! How you and the team turn crises into opportunities. You'll speak to your superior in terms of increased sales growth, new business opportunities, and greater return on investment.

Isn't all of this better than walking in unprepared and nervously waiting for your boss to pick you apart and then tell you that there won't be much of an increase for you this year?

When you are *this* prepared, negotiation becomes easy because you've already done all the hard work. You put the onus squarely on your boss to come back with a decent offer.

Does this always work? No, nothing works all the time because life is seldom fair and never static; the economy changes, the industry is in depression and the Company is underfunded or lost a major Client - that's life; however, despite all of this, *you've* grown stronger!

And should the unfair thing happen, as often does, and despite your best efforts, you still don't get that salary increase - it will be different from prior years because now you have choices; you can stay if you choose or move on to bigger and better opportunities because you are smarter and more accomplished. The best part is that you get to take all those accomplishments with you.

So never forget, you are always working for yourself!

Action Steps

1. Know what you need and want, and identify what issues you are prepared to compromise on for a specific upside later on.

   When it comes to remuneration - you should have a range based on what you absolutely need (the bare minimum) and what you would ideally like (the top end of the range); then see whether the offer that you have been presented with fits within the range and is acceptable to you.

2. Demonstrate that you are flexible and accommodating. Show that you are prepared to compromise and are able to contribute immediately!

3. Show that you care about the Company and that being in the right organization and being able to contribute value to your employer is more important to you than money.

   Never let your employer think that you are *only* about money and what's in it for you!

CHAPTER 12

Onboarding - Additional Strategies For A Seamless Transition To Your New Position

"The secret to change is to focus all of your energy not on fighting the old, but on building the new."

Socrates

A few years ago, I was taking a course in Executive Search, to further hone my skills and keep up to date with new developments - I am a lifelong learner and am always looking to learn from others, irrespective of knowing the process inside out and having international experience.

I never let that cloud my judgement, nor do I allow myself to think I know more than other Executive Search Professionals - on the contrary, I believe one should always keep an open mind to learn as much as possible.

The trainer giving the course was a crusty "old boy" who I neither knew nor had ever heard of before, but he had some impressive marketing material and I fell for his course. He also still had an active Search Firm with Consultants doing Executive Search for his Clients, so he was still involved in the practice on a daily basis, in addition to training.

During one of his lectures, I asked what he would do if he had placed a Candidate who did not show up on the first day of work.

Fortunately, this has never happened to me - but I think that's because I really prepare down to the last detail and believe in communicating with my Candidates and simply being there for them if they need anything. However, I was particularly interested in his response because his attitude was quite different from mine.

His response to my question: "That's NOT *my* problem!"

"How could it *not* be your problem?" I argued. "You have just charged a Client 30% of the Candidate's total compensation, and you're telling me that if the Candidate does not show up - it's not *your* problem?"

"Yes!' he said, "The Client is paying me to *find* Candidates - and that's what I did - I gave them a selection of shortlisted Candidates (two by the way!) And they chose a Candidate (he never sat in on the finalist interviews - so he was neither as interested nor as invested as I was) and if that Candidate does not show up, it's not *my* problem!"

I was mortified, and decided then and there that I prefer the way I do business!

I really want my Candidates and my Clients to know how much I care, and the reason I mention this story is that for me, the Search Assignment does not end when the Candidate that I placed starts working for my Client. No, it ends when the Candidate is successful in their position and the Client is thrilled with their new hire.

When a Candidate joins a new Company, we call this "Onboarding" - Wikipedia's definition is as follows, and I think it is a very eloquent and precise explanation:

Onboarding also known as organizational socialization refers to the mechanism through which new employees acquire the necessary knowledge, skills, and behaviors to become effective organizational members and insiders.[1]

Onboarding has become an entire specialization in itself, and it would be remiss of me if I did not discuss it and give you guidance to make the first year of your transition as easy as possible.

The statistics are staggering and dismal. According to an article published by Forbes, almost 40% of new Senior Hires fail within their first 18 months.[2]

The primary reasons cited are:

1. A poor fit or match with the Company or position
2. Expectations on either side not being met, i.e. the Client expected more from the Candidate and the Candidate expected the Company to be more supportive.

My take on why so many new Executive Hires fail is simple: it always comes down to Strategy and Planning.

Let's focus a moment on "Strategy" and the two primary reasons given for failure:

1. A poor fit and
2. Unmet expectations on either side

If you have taken my advice to heart that Corporate Culture *is* your highest priority when deciding *who* you wish to work for. And, if you have followed my guidelines on exactly *how* to determine a Company's Corporate Culture and which one you'd fit best in, then you have already greatly minimized the risk of "being a poor fit" with your next Employer.

---

[1] "Onboarding - Wikipedia, the free encyclopedia." 2011. 4 Sep. 2015 <https://en.wikipedia.org/wiki/Onboarding>

[2] "Executive Onboarding: The Key to Accelerating Success and." 2012. 4 Sep. 2015 <http://www.forbes.com/sites/georgebradt/2012/02/15/executive-onboarding-the-key-to-accelerating-success-and-reducing-risk-in-a-new-job/>

Let's look at reason number two: Unmet expectations on either side.

I will guide you through the maze of these unchartered waters to ensure a seamless and enjoyable transition as we plan for your success. Expectations are often predicated on two specific things:

1. What you assume others will or should do for you, and

2. Communication - how often, openly, and honestly they tell you what you need to know

Planning For Your Ascendency

There is a period of time from when you've signed your new offer to the time that you actually start working. W*hat* you choose to do during this period of time is crucial to your success!

You may be in a situation where you are still employed or you may be in-between-jobs and are enjoying some free time before you step into your next role. Whatever your situation, I want you to carve out some time to do Planning.

That's right! Planning! - By now you should know that I would never let you leave anything to chance and just "mosey-on-into" your next Executive position. Not if you are one of my Candidates. Oh No! - I am much too invested in your success, and besides I have a reputation to look after.

What to do once you have the position, but before you officially start

1. Find out who the most important stakeholders will be. Most of this information you will already know, but please do not take anything for granted - building relationships and forging great alliances are going to be crucial to your success.

2. I want you to make a list of all the people who are important and in a position to help you:

   - Your immediate Superior

   - Your immediate Superior's Executive PA

- A Senior Person within HR who will possibly be your "Liaison" and can give you incredible insights into the various "Power Players" and put you in touch with the right people

- Your Colleagues, and

- Direct reports

- Important Stakeholders, such as Members of the Board of Directors that you have not yet met, the Company's Bankers and don't forget the External Auditors (that may be a first for many of them!) - but who better to talk to than the External Auditors, to give you a valuable assessment on exactly how the Company is doing and what their biggest challenges are?

   If you are either the new CFO or CEO, then this will be one of the most important relationships that you will have to manage - so start early!

3. Once you have gone over that list and prioritized which people you ought to meet first, then reach out to them individually and take them out to lunch, so that you can have some one-on-one time with them. This will help you immensely to create great rapport, build a relationship, and help you strategize for specific milestones and early wins.

   Depending on your level of Seniority - you should do the same with your Superior or key Members of the Board of Directors. Personal perspectives and insights can be invaluable when it comes to developing your "Plan of Action" for the challenges that lie ahead.

The First Six Months

You will be watched like a hawk for the first six months, so this period is going to be exceptionally important to you, your Superior(s), and your Direct reports.

You'll need to be proactive and do the following:

1. Draw up a strategy for the challenges you have to meet

2. Timeline those milestones, and have a detailed plan with all the necessary resources that you will need

3. Prioritize, measure, and evaluate

4. Be specific, precise, and absolutely clear with your expectations

5. Keep communicating to all Stakeholders and your key people. In return, ask for their feedback

6. When you achieve those goals, especially the early "wins" - Celebrate with your team and give *them* credit.

© Randy Glasbergen
glasbergen.com

"I always give 110% to my job —
40% on Monday, 30% on Tuesday, 20% on
Wednesday, 15% on Thursday and 5% on Friday."

Companies Are Seeing The Value Of Having An Onboarding Strategy for Senior Hires

As the success of any new Hire benefits both the Executive and the Company - many companies are investing in having a formal Onboarding Strategy.

This may include, but is not limited to, the following:

1. Having an "Interim" person to help lead and guide the newly hired Executive through the hurdles and nuances of the Company, build strategic relationships and even inducting them into the Company's Corporate Culture, so that the new Executive assimilates as quickly as possible.

2. Outlining expectations of the role and setting goals and timelines for the achievement of those goals

3. Defining what success looks like and establishing the resources necessary to make that happen

4. Providing Leadership Coaching Courses and often providing or paying for an Executive Coach to assist the new Executive with their transition

There are many ways that companies are investing in the Onboarding Phase because it is obviously a win for both the Candidate and the Client, and success is always a collaborative effort!

I gave you these guidelines as you may find a position with a Company that does *not* have a formal policy in place for Onboarding their new Executives.

You have to be proactive and take charge of your own Career.

Learn as much as you can and do get a Business or Executive Career Coach; sign up for a course to help you transition as successfully as you can. This may be one of the best investments you ever make!

Action Steps

1. Have a strategy to meet corporate objectives for the:

   - First 3 months

   - First 6 months

   - One Year Anniversary

2. Always keep the lines of communication open, encourage people to come to you, be open to their feedback, and encourage them to talk in a non-judgmental environment, which engenders trust.

   Build strategic alliances amongst all stakeholders - you can never have too many advocates.

   Establish early wins amongst your staff and celebrate them openly. Be generous with your praise. No single character trait will engender more admiration and respect from your staff in your leadership abilities and self confidence in theirs!

3. Lead by serving. Your leadership style speaks volumes about your character. By acknowledging others and giving credit to your team, you inspire others to want to follow and work with you.

CHAPTER 13

Putting It
All Together

"The best revenge is massive success."

Frank Sinatra

This has been quite a trip, and for old time's sake, I'd like to look back on how far you've travelled, starting with the insights you've gained and the lessons learned.

In Chapter 2, you found out that no limiting belief has the power to hold you back - if you simply make up your mind to take action and do what you need to do!

At our next landmark, Chapter 3, you found out that in order to get what *you* want, you need to shift the paradigm and give a prospective Employer what *they* want first!

You delved deep to uncover your greatest strengths by making *yourself* your most important project.

Once you had figured out how utterly amazing you are, by knowing what you *love* doing and reliving the memories of your considerable achievements, you *know* you *are* the *best* Candidate for the job because you have so much to offer and you can *contribute immediately!*

After we'd passed through Chapter 4, you had a much better idea of how the industry works and how the different players have contrasting agendas. Knowing *this* puts you in a much more informed position, but the most important thing you learned by far - is that you have choices!

You found out that you could truly be in a power position, instead of handing your power over to a third party that does not necessarily have *your* best interests at heart.

Chapter 5 you cruised through while observing and learning how an Executive Search Process really works, taking the mystery out as to what happens, and why things sometimes take so long.

In Chapter 6, things started getting interesting; you learned first-hand how critical planning is and what you could expect from a prospective Employer.

You learned how they will initially engage you through the different forms of Social Media, and what you need to do to present yourself to best advantage for every medium and at every stage.

Then we stopped to rest a while because Chapter 7 was the real crux of the process - "The Interview" - where you learned exactly what to do, and more specifically, what *not* to do!

You were shown that in order to Ace your Interview, you have to be authentic, nice to everyone you meet, and know precisely what you are looking for, and most importantly, *what* you have to offer.

Our trip continued with Chapter 8 when you realized the importance of saying "Thank You" and being grateful.

In Chapter 9, you learned that, even though the interview was over, you were far from done. However impressed the Search Committee was with your performance, now it was *their* turn to